s / Number 04-003

Freshman Representatives and the Learning of Voting Cues

HERBERT B. ASHER
Ohio State University

SAGE PUBLICATIONS / Beverly Hills / London

For information address:

SAGE PUBLICATIONS, INC.
275 South Beverly Drive
Beverly Hills, California 90212

SAGE PUBLICATIONS, INC.
St George's House / 44 Hatton Garden
London EC1N 8ER

International Standard Book Number 0-8039-0262-x

Library of Congress Catalog Card No. L.C. 73-80259

FIRST PRINTING

When citing a professional paper, please use the proper form. Remember to cite the
correct Sage Professional Paper series title and include the paper number. One of the
two following formats can be adapted (depending on the style manual used):

(1) NAGEL, S. S. (1973) Comparing Elected and Appointed Judicial Systems. Sage
    Professional Paper in American Politics 04-001. Beverly Hills and London:
    Sage Pubns.

OR

(2) Nagel, Stuart S., *Comparing Elected and Appointed Judicial Systems.* Beverly
    Hills and London: Sage Professional Paper in American Politics 04-001, 1973.

CONTENTS

Freshman Representatives and
the Learning of Voting Cues

HERBERT B. ASHER
Ohio State University

INTRODUCTION

Observers have often noted that congressmen are called upon to vote on a
great number of bills spanning highly disparate substantive areas. It has
been suggested that representatives must therefore employ some econo-
mizing device in order to cope with this tremendous decisional burden.
One such shortcut procedure with great intuitive appeal is the reliance
upon fellow congressmen in areas where the representative is unsure,
uninformed, or even indifferent. This reliance is commonly referred to as
cue-taking. Given that members do depend heavily on their legislative
colleagues, there emerges a key question of how these patterns of reliance
develop. In short, how do congressmen learn the best sources for
information and advice in a voting situation? Do representatives learn
where to turn for voting cues over time, either beginning with no
cue-givers in mind or changing from initial dependence on certain
cue-givers to later reliance on others? Or do representatives stay with an
initial set of cue-givers? Under what conditions do legislators' cue sources
change or remain the same?

AUTHOR'S NOTE: *I am particularly indebted to Aage Clausen and Herb Weisberg
for their helpful advice on all aspects of the paper and to John Kingdon for his many
contributions to the dissertation chapter from which this paper is in part drawn. It
was Lutz Erbring who brought to my attention the mode of cluster analysis
employed herein, a much appeciated contribution. John Kessel's comments on the
paper and Richard Hofstetter's suggestions on the roll call analysis are also
appreciated.*

These questions are best answered by an investigation of freshman congressmen, those legislative novices most likely to be undergoing cue-learning. Hence, two major data bases are used in this paper: a panel study of the freshman representatives elected to the Ninety-First Congress and a cluster bloc analysis of the same congress with emphasis on the blocs in which newcomers appeared.[1] Before turning to the data analysis, some general comments about applications of the cue transmission idea are in order.

ESTIMATION AND SIMULATION MODELS OF LEGISLATIVE VOTING

The cue transmission idea has been incorporated in regression and simulation models of legislative voting. Two works in the former category are Jackson's (1969) study of Senate voting and Mishler et al.'s (1973) analysis of cue-taking by freshman representatives. Both studies employ as independent variables a set of cue-givers internal and external to the legislative body. The utility of these and other estimation models in predicting vote outcomes is impressive (as reflected in substantial R^2s), but their explanatory power is less impressive because the actual processes whereby the legislator decides how to vote can at best only be inferred from these models. For example, a party leadership variable may be a good predictor of how a member votes, but the reasons why a legislator is in voting agreement with his leadership remain unknown.

Simulation models of legislative decision-making and voting appear to hold the greater promise for describing the processes involved in legislative cue transmission since they often attempt to portray the actual processes of interpersonal interaction. The most explicit statement of the cue-giving model has been given by Matthews and Stimson (1969a; 1969b) in two papers that also present the basic results of their simulation.[2] Their fundamental assertion, similar to that of other investigators, is that somehow representatives make decisions about a whole range of complex issues; the question is how. After reviewing and criticizing a number of models appropriate to legislative voting, Matthews and Stimson conclude that it is the cue-giving model that is most appropriate since it does not require the representative to carry out any extensive information collection and evaluation. They write:

> We hypothesize that when a member is confronted with the necessity of casting a roll call vote on a complex issue about which

he knows very little, he searches for cues provided by trusted colleagues who—because of their formal position in the legislature or policy specialization—have more information than he does and with whom he would probably agree if he had the time and information to make an independent decision. Cue-givers need not be individuals. When overwhelming majorities of groups which the member respects and trusts—the whole House, the members of his party or state delegation, for example—vote the same way the member is likely to accept their collective judgment as his own [Matthews and Stimson, 1969a: 11].

Assuming that Matthews and Stimson have provided a useful explanation of much of legislative voting, their operationalization of it via a computer simulation leaves many questions unanswered. While the accurate predictions resulting from the simulation are consistent with the cue-giving model, the simulation does not account for differing patterns of cue receptivity and transmission, mainly because there are no processes formally built into the simulation. Matthews and Stimson recognized this problem in an updated version of their earlier paper:

To say that cue-taking is the "normal" process of decision for House members is merely the beginning of a better understanding of decision-making by the House of Representatives. The conditions under which "abnormal" decision-strategies are followed must be further specified. Why rank and file member "A" follows specialist "B" rather than specialist "C", how cues are transmitted, why members choose to specialize in one area rather than another, and many more unanswered questions spring to mind [Matthews and Stimson, 1969b: 17].

The Shapiro (1968) simulation also incorporates cue-taking and is more explicitly process-oriented. Each representative is assigned a predisposition score on a bill according to a number of criteria; if this score is not judged to be of sufficient magnitude to cause the member to vote yes or no on that bill, then he enters the communications phase. But the manner in which numerical assignments were made to the components of the model, especially in the communication phase, leads one to wonder whether the simulation truly reflects legislative processes. Wherever possible, Shapiro refers to some legislative literature in fixing certain parameters, but the literature cited is sketchy and often not directly about the House. For example, probabilities are assigned to conversations that the rank and file member of the House might have, but a .04 probability of talking with a fellow party member, a .01 probability of talking with a member of the opposite party, or a .3 probability of talking with a colleague on one's state delegation is certainly not rooted in any solid empirical foundation.

One must ask whether changing these values would alter the results or whether indeed these values are at all reasonable. Furthermore, the communication phase adds little to the predictive power of the simulation for the roll calls being simulated, nor do we know how well the communication phase alone would predict. We do know that when one roll call vote (HR 11926) is excluded from the simulation, the "just party" model predicts almost as well as the full model—82.5% versus 84% accuracy in predictions[3]—perhaps suggesting that on grounds of parsimony the elaborated model be dismissed, particularly given the frailty of its empirical underpinnings. Thus, even a simulation that includes interactive stages may not be reflecting processes very accurately.

There are some general issues associated with simulation models of legislative voting; one of these concerns the validation of the models. Accurate prediction is certainly not sufficient to conclude that a model is representing the underlying patterns of behavior. A high level of prediction tells us only about outcomes; we must still infer the processes. If a model failed even to predict well, we might then dismiss it as uninteresting. Of course, two or more models may possess comparable predictive powers, although based on markedly divergent process theories. The choice between models then becomes a decision transcending the data: a variety of other factors must be taken into account, including the plausibility of each model and its generalizability. Oftentimes the selection of one model over another must await additional information, such as interview material obtained directly from the relevant actors.

Yet another comment about legislative decision-making simulations is that they appear to be applicable mainly to routine issues; yet it is the non-routine, often controversial, rancorous issue that is often of primary interest to the political scientist. The basic rationale for the Matthews and Stimson model is that representatives need a shortcut in order to make reasonable decisions on a multitude of issues about which they could not possibly be fully informed. Their argument seems very convincing for most issues; but on issues hotly debated in the public arena or on questions vital to his district and hence his electoral future, the representative seems very likely to collect the material needed to make an informed and purposive decision. In fact, Matthews and Stimson (1969a: 28-29) observe that the largest source of error in their predictions was the situation of conflicting cues; here their predictions were little better than chance.

A number of additional criteria are used to evaluate a simulation, but these are not central to our purposes. What is important is that most models of legislative voting, even process-oriented simulations, demand additional data in order to delineate the underlying processes. A potentially informative set of materials would be over-time interviews with the legislative actors undergoing cue-learning. It is to this topic that we now turn with an eye toward how the freshman members of the Ninety-First Congress learned voting cues.

FRESHMAN CUE RESPONSES

INTRODUCTION

At the first wave of interviews (t_1), the freshman replies to the cues questions were very tentative, hesitant, and uncertain, suggesting that a lot of learning was yet to take place.[4] This basic finding would seem to contradict the assertion by Mishler et al. (1973: 396) that freshman representatives upon entering the House "have already mastered appropriate low information strategies [i.e., cue-taking] of decision irrespective of the extent of their familiarity with legislative custom and ritual." If Mishler et al. are simply stating that freshmen are willing to take cues from the very beginning of their service, then they are undoubtedly correct. But it appears that they are claiming that newcomers are both willing *and* able to engage in cue-taking, a conclusion that cannot be demonstrated by their data and analysis technique. Examining the roll calls of an entire congressional session excludes the possibility that freshmen may have undergone substantial learning in the early months of that session. Furthermore, the sizable R^2s obtained by their regression analysis do not prove that particular causal relationships hold; alternative explanations may have the same high level of predictive power.[5]

It is not surprising that the responses to the cues items revealed such uncertainty at t_1. The questions demanded a specific type of information from the representative: he had to cite actual names of House colleagues, often in reference to specific issue areas. While the names of the party leadership and delegation dean would likely be known by the freshman, other names such as committee chairmen and ranking minority members, representatives with special areas of expertise, and members with similar districts and ideologies to the freshman's might all be unknown to the newcomer and probably have to be learned over time.

Another factor that contributed to the tentativeness of the t_1 responses was the almost complete absence of any votes, roll call or otherwise, at the first wave of interviewing. This is generally true for the early stages of all congresses, but was especially pronounced for the Ninety-First which proceeded at a very slow pace in its early months, partly because of the change in control of the executive branch. This means that there were few concrete issues and bills about which to question the freshmen, a situation that has a number of implications as noted by Kingdon (1969) in his discussion of the use of survey instruments in studying legislative behavior:

> In the study of legislative voting or other decision-making, the basic exercise which would usually be demanded of a respondent by using this procedure [a standard survey instrument] is that he take himself out of the concrete context within which he makes his decisions and abstract or generalize about the process. This exercise encounters a number of difficulties, whether the interview is structured or unstructured.
>
> First, a respondent under such circumstances may speak in terms of generalizations which may or may not have a great deal of relationship to his actual votes. . . . These general notions that legislators have about their work may be quite crucial in explaining their behavior, but there is little that interviews about the general decision process can do to discover whether and under what conditions they are important.
>
> The second problem . . . is the reputational problem. It is tempting for a respondent to slip into judging the reputations of others in the legislative system rather than their actual influence.
>
> Finally, active participants in a process often find it difficult to step back from their activities and abstract about the process. . . . The closer the interview is to the actual context within which the decision-maker is operating, the more valid the results will be [Kingdon, 1969: 4-5].

Two basic kinds of questions were asked in collecting information about freshman cue-learning. The first might be called context questions: the freshmen were asked whom they might turn to for information and advice in a variety of voting situations ranging from general to bill-specific. The other kind of question inquired directly about the importance of a number of possible cue-givers. First the responses to the contextual questions will be examined for both t_1 and t_2 to be followed by an analysis of the replies to the items about specific cue-givers.

CUE TRANSMISSION IN A VARIETY OF SITUATIONS

Cue-Taking in an Undefined Situation

The freshman congressmen were first asked if there were any representatives to whom they would generally turn for information and advice on matters that came before the House.[6] The question was deliberately phrased in general terms, divorced from any specific issue context, so as to clearly differentiate those newcomers with specific cue-givers in mind from those without any.

The responses to this item at t_1 were often tentative, as one might expect. Ten freshmen at t_1 said that there will be such members, but that it was too early in their legislative careers to cite specific names. Some typical responses were:

> There will be people that I'll turn to. I'll probably go to the ranking minority members of the committees.

> Not yet. I haven't been here long enough yet. I've heard that members depend a great deal on fellow party members on committees.

> I haven't been here long enough to really say, but I'd turn to people with expertise and people whom I had confidence in.

The state delegation was the most frequently cited source of general advice early in the freshman's legislative career. Of the 28 responses to this general query at t_1, 11 included specific references to individual legislators or groups of legislators. The state delegation was mentioned on 8 of these 11 responses; there are various reasons for this. Most of the Ninety-First Congress newcomers said that they had worked through their delegation, particularly the senior member from their party, in obtaining their committee assignments. Some delegations with freshman representatives held meetings early in the Ninety-First, even before the committees got down to serious work. In addition, the congressmen that freshmen were most likely to know prior to entering the House were members of their delegation. Six freshmen mentioned the party leadership including the speaker, majority and minority leaders and whips, and chairman of the Republican Conference; and 5 referred to committee members in general or by name. It is noteworthy that more than half of the freshmen unable to name specific cue-givers at t_1 did expect committee contacts to become influential in the future.

At t_2, the responses to this general query were far more detailed; 15 of 24 freshmen could now cite names and groups. One Republican newcomer literally rattled off 11 names including the party leadership, members of his state party delegation, fellow committee members, and a freshman colleague. Another Republican who at t_1 had no idea to whom he would turn listed three names at t_2, explaining that these three men were "from an area with similar problems to mine and with a similar philosophy." Two southern Democratic freshmen without any general cue-givers at t_1 did name some at t_2 and explained their choices as influenced mainly by regional factors. One said, "You are greatly influenced by geographical and philosophical considerations. This is especially true of southerners who more than any other group share a common philosophy." Ten members at t_2 referred to their state delegation, while the number of committee references jumped to 12 from 5, undoubtedly a reflection of the salience of committees and committee work as the tempo of the Ninety-First Congress increased. Three of the 24 freshmen at t_2 still said without qualification that there was no one on whom they would generally rely, while 6 others gave vague responses that were difficult to interpret as references to specific cue-givers or not. Hence, the responses to the general query at t_1 and t_2 clearly indicate cue-learning, although the patterns of cue acquisition remain to be elucidated.

One final comment about state party delegations is appropriate at this point. The size of the state party delegation had little relation to the frequency of delegation mentions. That is, freshmen from large delegations were no more likely to refer to fellow party delegation members than newcomers from small delegations that included at least one fellow party member. Furthermore, freshmen from more "cohesive" delegations, as defined by Deckard (1972), were no more likely to cite fellow party delegation members than freshmen from less cohesive delegations. This latter result should not be assigned too much weight as there were only 9 freshmen interviewed who came from the state party delegations discussed by Deckard. Thus, membership in a large state delegation does not account for the patterns of cue references uncovered, at least not for the Ninety-First Congress freshmen. The impact of the state delegation will be considered in much greater detail later.

Cue-Taking Within General Issue Areas

It was expected that the extent of cue-learning would vary across substantive areas with the greatest learning occurring for those issues domains that were of least concern and familiarity to the newcomer. Hence, the freshmen were asked to consider three general issue areas—civil rights, domestic policy, and foreign affairs[7]—and to state the areas in which they were most and least likely to consult with other members. The expectation was that freshmen would cite other members most frequently in the area of foreign affairs, mainly because of its lesser saliency in most districts and its probable lesser immediacy to most congressmen. For just the opposite reasons, it was expected that civil rights would be the area exhibiting the lowest incidence of cue-taking. These expectations held only weakly at t_1, but were far more pronounced at t_2 as indicated in Table 1.

TABLE 1
ISSUE AREAS OF GREATEST AND LEAST CONSULTATIONS

	t_1	t_1-adjusted[a]	t_2
Area Most Likely to Consult			
Dom. Pol.	6	6	4
For. Pol.	9	6	13
Civil Rights	4	4	2
All	7	6	3
D.K.	2	0	0
Area Least Likely to Consult			
Dom. Pol.	5	5	5
For. Pol.	7	7	4
Civil Rights	8	5	10
All	5	4	3
D.K.	3	1	0

a. The adjusted t_1 figures include only those freshmen interviewed at both t_1 and t_2.

Considering only freshmen interviewed at both t_1 and t_2, we can see that there is a doubling in the frequency of responses citing foreign affairs as the area of greatest consultation and civil rights as the area of least. Members gave two main reasons for consulting in foreign affairs: a lack of expertise in this area and a recognition of its lesser importance to the district which meant fewer and more ambiguous constituency directives in this domain. Civil rights was viewed as an area in which expertise was less important because the members' own attitudes and beliefs were thought sufficient to make a decision. In addition, civil rights was perceived as a very salient issue to the district, especially to northern urban districts with sizable black populations and to southern constituencies. Constituency preferences were clear in this domain, and the freshman had less need and desire to obtain advice from other congressmen. Presumably, then, an investigation of cue transmission in legislative voting would be most rewarding for foreign affairs issues and least profitable for civil rights legislation where the members' choices are largely dictated by external pressures. Thus, even if we observe southern representatives voting together on civil rights matters, this does not prove that cues internal to the House were transmitted; southern members may instead be responding in a similar fashion to common constituency pressures.

The freshmen were also asked at both t_1 and t_2 whether there were any particular congressmen to whom they would turn for information on civil rights, foreign policy, and domestic legislation. An interesting result occurred here. Although foreign policy was the area in which freshmen were most likely to consult, it was also the area in which they were least able to mention specific representatives or groups as possible sources of information at t_1. Again, this can probably be explained by the lower saliency of foreign policy matters to the freshmen, as well as their unfamiliarity with the House Foreign Affairs Committee. This led us to expect that the greatest learning of cues from t_1 to t_2 would be in the area of foreign affairs, and this is confirmed in Table 2.

There are several points to be made about Table 2. First, as expected, the greatest incidence of cue-learning occurred in the area of foreign affairs. In particular, the House Foreign Affairs Committee became much more visible to the freshmen with 6 different members of the committee being mentioned in various responses. For 2 freshmen at t_2, obtaining information on foreign policy matters became very simplified: one looked to the ranking Republican on the committee who was also from the freshman's home state, while the other newcomer looked to the chairman of the committee who was also the dean of his state delegation. The combination of delegation ties and committee membership is indeed a very powerful one, and it is often difficult to disentangle the impact of each.

There appeared to be little cue-learning over time in domestic affairs, as evidenced by the fact that 12 freshmen at both t_1 and t_2 named specific representatives or groups as possible sources of information. And in the domain of civil rights, there was actually a decrease in the number of references to other members. This occurred because two southern freshmen (a Democrat and a Republican) who had named their respective party leaderships as sources of information and advice on civil rights legislation at t_1, reported at t_2 that they would not turn to anyone in particular. This may be due to their "learning" that constituency cues were so clear and constraining that consultation with other members was unnecessary. Another explanation for not turning to anyone in particular for cues on civil rights matters is that members can look to almost

TABLE 2

CUE-LEARNING IN THREE ISSUE AREAS OVER TIME[a]

Freshmen Citing Specific Individuals or Groups (n)	t_1	t_1-adjusted	t_2
Civil Rights	11	11	9
Foreign Policy	6	5	13
Domestic Policy	15	12	12

a. Because of the broadness of the domestic category, any response that said "yes" to consultation depending on the committee from which the bill originated was considered as referring to a specific individual or group.

everyone in the House for cues in this field, since it was often perceived as not requiring special expertise.

Cue-Taking on Specific Policy Questions

The discussion to this point has focused on freshman responses to items that were divorced from the context of specific issues. Such questions may impose too great a strain on the newcomer's ability to project his likely behavior. Thus, the freshmen were asked about possible cue-givers in the context of specific votes, a situation that moves us closer to the newcomer's actual behavior. At t_1 there were two issues that seemed profitable to investigate—the leadership battles in each party[8] and the votes on the seating of Adam Clayton Powell. These two issues evoked widely disparate patterns of response. The leadership votes came very early in the session and required Democratic and Republican freshmen (especially the latter) to choose between men they did not know. Committees had not yet met nor had freshmen had any extensive opportunity to meet and interact with many senior members of their party. Therefore, the most likely source of information for the newcomer was his own state party delegation, and this is confirmed in the interview responses. Eleven freshmen referred to the state delegation as being of assistance in the leadership votes, while 16 said that they had turned to no one for advice. But only 4 freshmen mentioned the state delegation in reference to the Powell votes, while 25 said that they turned to no one at all. In fact, a number of freshmen claimed to have voted in the Powell affair opposite to the direction in which significant forces were pushing them. One newcomer said that he was the only Democratic member of his sizable state party delegation to vote against Powell's seating. Two members said that they based their vote on constitutional grounds, while two said they had made their decision even before entering congress. Another freshman said, "This was a case where my mind was made up and I did not want the facts to confuse things." Thus, in the leadership votes, there was fairly extensive reliance on internal House cues, especially the state delegation, while in the Powell vote there was minimal reliance on House cues.

Clearly, these varying patterns arose because of the nature of the issues involved. One was an issue confined to the House arena—to be decided by House members largely independent of external pressures. The other was a public issue, an emotional issue that generated intense feeling in the districts which in turn reduced the influence that internal House cues might have. The differences in these issues have obvious consequences for the cue-giving model of legislative voting. On routine issues that require information, but are not controversial outside the House, the cue-giving model appears both realistic and useful. But on issues that generate controversy outside the House setting, one must widen the set of possible influences on the congressman.

At t_2, freshmen were queried about 5 more votes: the raising of the debt ceiling, the Elementary and Secondary Education Act (ESEA), the name change for the House Committee on Un-American Activities (HUAC), funding for the International Development Agency (IDA), and (at that time) the forthcoming ABM vote.[9] Table 3 presents the pattern of cue responses for these 5 votes by party.

Cue references on the HUAC vote were infrequent. While the issue did generate some controversy, it was not one that freshmen perceived to be very consequential. Two newcomers said that "the whole thing was silly." But the situation with respect to the debt ceiling and IDA funding votes was substantially different, with Republican freshmen exhibiting a much greater incidence of cue-taking. The reason for this is straightforward: both measures were strongly advocated by the Republican administration, yet were issues on which many Republican freshmen philosophically

TABLE 3
CUE-GIVERS CITED FOR FIVE ROLL CALL VOTES[a]

Cue-Giver	HUAC		IDA		Debt		ESEA		ABM		Total
	R	D	R	D	R	D	R	D	R	D	
State delegation	2	0	1	0	0	2	2	3	1	1	12
Committee member	0	2	2	1	1	0	9	4	1	3	23
Party leadership	0	0	2	0	4	1	0	1	0	0	8
President-administration	0	0	2	0	3	0	0	0	4	0	9
Regional colleague	0	0	0	1	0	0	1	0	1	0	3
Ideological colleague	0	1	1	1	0	2	0	2	0	0	7
General discussion	0	0	2	0	3	0	1	1	0	0	7
Subtotal	2	3	10	3	11	5	13	11	7	4	69
Total	5		13		16		24		11		69

a. More than one cue for each respondent for each vote was coded so that the total N for each vote need not add up to the number of freshmen interviewed at t_2. In most cases, the total N for a vote is less than the number of freshmen, implying that many newcomers cited no cue-givers on that vote. Where a menioned representative was both a relevant committee member and a member of the freshman's state delegation, he was coded in both categoreis. A representative was placed in the regional and ideological categories only if he was not a member of the newcomer's state delegation, of the committee in question, or of the party leadership. DSG and other informal groups were not coded because so few references to them per se were made, and because membership lists of these groups were often unavailable.

preferred to vote no and would have done so had there been a Democratic administration in power. Many Republican freshmen were cross-pressured; the leadership recognized their plight and attempted to structure the issues as party issues. One GOP newcomer said about the debt ceiling vote:

> I talked with a hell of a lot of people about it, with anybody and everybody. I voted to raise the ceiling. But I stated publicly that this would be the last time that I would vote to raise the ceiling in the absence of all-out war, Nixon or no Nixon.

A conservative Republican freshman said that the debt ceiling "was an administration problem and I went along with them." Another asserted, "We don't have much choice; the President needed it." An eastern freshman said that "this was the prime example of a party issue." Because the debt ceiling vote was a party issue for Republican freshmen (but not for Democrats), it is not surprising that the preponderance of their responses referred to the party leadership and the President. A similar situation held for the IDA vote, although it did not appear to generate as much inner turmoil for Republican freshmen. But even here, two GOP newcomers recognized that they voted against the administration and a third asserted in very moralistic terms that he "could not swallow it."

The vote with the greatest frequency of cue-taking for both parties was the Elementary and Secondary Education Act, with the predominant pattern being references to members of the Education and Labor Committee. The basic question involved was the type of renewal there would be in the existing education legislation: whether there would be a five-year renewal as advocated by the Democratic leadership, or a three-year renewal as proposed in the Quie (R.-Minnesota)-Green (D.-Oregon) amendment largely supported by the Republican leadership. The particular member mentioned most often by Democratic freshmen was Carl Perkins, chairman of Education and Labor; while Republican newcomers referred most frequently to Albert Quie, cosponsor of the aforementioned amendment and second-ranking Republican on Education and Labor. Thus, we had here an issue for freshmen that was partisan in nature, but that also posed informational problems for them in the sense of their having to decide between alternative versions of a bill rather than merely voting a single bill up or down. When the informational problem enters the scene, there is a strong reliance on members of the committee from which the bill originated, a result fully consistent with the literature on committees.

The final issue presented to the freshmen concerned the forthcoming ABM vote. Because the issue at that time was still some way from the voting stage, some of the responses were tentative and vague. Republican freshmen unsure of their ultimate vote tended to perceive the ABM as a partisan issue, as a question of support for the President. Thus, their most common cue reference was to the President and the administration. For Democrats uncertain of their vote, and not bound by partisan loyalty to the President, the ABM matter was viewed primarily as an informational question centered on the feasibility of the system; hence, their responses were oriented mainly to the Armed Services Committee.

Thus far, cue-taking has been studied in relation to general issue areas and specific votes. Although substantial cue-taking was observed, it is important to recognize that a half or more of the freshmen never mentioned any cue-givers in the House at either t_1 or t_2. Thus, there appears to be an inconsistency between the findings presented herein and the stronger claims for the cue-giving model made by Matthews and Stimson. However, it is possible that the discrepancy can be accounted for, or at least minimized, by considering other ways in which the cue-giving model may occur.

It is not mandatory that members formally converse with one another. A representative might merely listen to the alphabetic call of the roll and then vote the way that a member he trusts has voted. For example, a nonfreshman legislator said that if he voted opposite to the way that the member who preceded him in the alphabet did, he would have voted 95% of the time the same way he would have had he painstakingly gathered and evaluated information on each individual issue. Thus, cue-giving need not involve face-to-face conversations, yet the questions employed herein were phrased so as to inquire about personal exchanges of information—which meant that the rate of cue-giving uncovered was necessarily lower than would have been observed if a more liberal definition of cue-giving had been used.

But an even more important reason for the low incidence of cue-taking was the slow pace of the Ninety-First Congress mentioned earlier. At t_1, few measures had reached the voting stage; indeed many committees had not conducted any substantive legislative hearings. And even by t_2, the tempo of the Ninety-First Congress could best be described as leisurely. Issues were not springing up suddenly to catch the freshmen by surprise, but instead were coming up with ample advance warning. The pace of legislative activity has tremendous consequences for the usefulness of the cue-giving model. When members are bombarded by numerous matters all at once, or when issues arise unexpectedly, then cues will be very much needed as a simplifying mechanism.

The type of vote that seems best explained by recourse to cue transmission is the vote on an amendment introduced on the floor of the House to the bill under consideration. Such amendments are often disposed of immediately, thereby not allowing the member to collect independent information. He must rely on experts in the area, probably committee members, or colleagues that he trusts in order to make such quick decisions. As one freshman said at t_2:

> It is the amendments that pose a problem. You don't have time to contact the groups involved or your legislative assistant. Then you usually turn to someone on that committee whom you have confidence in.

Some freshmen were asked at t_2 the hypothetical question as to what they would do if they arrived on the House floor in the midst of a vote on a bill about which they were not fully informed.[10] This hypothetical situation was structured so as to be most favorable to the cue-giving model and this was reflected in the responses. Although only 11 freshmen were asked the question, 10 said that they would seek out either the party leadership, a member of their delegation, an appropriate committee member, or a trusted friend. It is noteworthy that only one freshman objected to this hypothetical situation by saying that it was unlikely to occur. Some illustrative responses were:

> I'd go to people whom I considered to be bellwethers. If I knew nothing about the bill, I'd ask someone I knew well enough whose answer I could trust and who would know where I would be on the bill.

> I'd quickly look around for "x" and "y" from my state and ask them about the bill. If it were an important bill, I would also ask Les and Gerry.

> I'd sit down at the leadership table. There are usually three to four fellows there-members of the Eighty-Ninth, Ninetieth and Ninety-First Clubs, and Gerry Ford.

> I'd get the bill, find out how the leadership feels, and ask the first representative that I had any confidence in about it. But I would not rely on only one opinion as he may be far out on that question.

> I'd pass on the first go-round and look for colleagues whose opinions I respect. I'd find out and come back in and vote on the second go-round.

Thus, although our information is not complete, it is clear that the cue-giving model is useful in accounting for voting in the House of Representatives. The information required in order to take cues from a fellow representative must be learned over time, and it is apparent that among the Ninety-First Congress freshmen the learning process was still going on at t_2. By t_2 there were freshmen representing the extremes of cue utilization. One liberal Democrat freshman had specific members to whom he would turn in each general issue domain; these always included relevant committee members as well as appropriate members of his sizable state party delegation. And on the specific votes surveyed, he consistently mentioned by name at least one member of the committee from which the bill originated as well as members of his delegation. Furthermore, his cue-givers were so well defined that the committee members cited clearly shared his ideological predispositions. For example, on the ABM question, he referred to members of the Armed Services Committee commonly perceived to be mavericks in terms of their support for military appropriations. At the other extreme were a number of freshmen who at t_2 were still saying that they did not know to whom they would turn in various situations. Presumably, a third wave of interviewing would have been required to unmask their cue-learning.

SUMMARY

The analysis suggests that a number of factors enter into a member's decision to take cues from a certain representative. Common party and state delegation membership, shared regional and ideological characteristics, reputations for accurate information, and expertise that is closely tied up with the committee system are all influential. In terms of ranking these possible sources of cues, certainly committee and state party delegation membership seem most important.

The gross patterns of cue-learning can be described as follows. Early in their careers, freshmen tend to rely on fellow party members in their state delegation since these are the men most likely to be known to the freshmen. With increased tenure in the House, even as soon as t_2 (four months later), patterns of cue-taking become more complex and more oriented to fellow party members on each of the committees. Where a fellow delegation member is also a member of the committee from which the bill originates, then the likelihood of his being a cue-giver is increased. A similar conclusion was reached by Arthur Stevens (1970: iii) in writing about congressmen in general:

> When they desire information about the provisions of legislation, they commonly turn to members of the committee which has jurisdiction. More specifically, Congressmen depend on those committee members who tend to share their own attitudinal predispositions and whom they know fairly well. Quite often these information sources are fellow state party delegation members.

These patterns say less about freshmen who do not enjoy the benefits of membership on sizable state delegations. Perhaps such freshmen employ compensatory strategies, probably in the form of a greater reliance on members from the same region or with similar districts as well as a greater reliance on ideologically compatible colleagues and, of course, appropriate committee members.

SOME INTERNAL HOUSE CUE-GIVERS

We have considered thus far general issue areas and specific issues, asking freshmen to specify potential and actual cue-givers. Our attention now shifts to the reasons for choices of cue-givers. Three possible sources of cues are investigated: the state delegation, the party leadership, and—for Republican freshmen—the President.

THE STATE PARTY DELEGATION

The importance of the state party delegation in voting situations and in general legislative interactions has been amply documented, particularly in roll call analyses. For example, Matthews and Stimson (1969a: 23) found in their simulation model:

> The consistently most important single cue-giver in both parties is the member's state party delegation—the average Democrat voting with his state party colleagues over 90 per cent of the time, the average Republican displaying the same pattern between 84 and 89 percent of the time.

Years earlier, David Truman (1959) concluded from a cluster bloc analysis that the state party delegation was important for legislative voting, although his conclusions were more tentative. In an earlier statement, Truman (1956: 1024) cogently argued that "in the absence of well-defined institutionalized, and continuously operative cue-giving mechanisms within the legislative party," a variety of informal devices would be employed by legislators in making voting decisions; one consequential device would be the state party delegation. In a very recent work based on agreement scores, Arthur Stevens (1970: 65-69) found substantial state party delegation unity, as did Kessel (1964), who also noted bipartisan delegation unity when state interests were at stake.

The special importance of the state party delegation for the freshman representative has also been well documented. Masters (1963: 36) observed that freshman committee assignments were most often channeled through the party delegation. Fiellin (1963: 67-68) saw the state delegation as being especially influential in the socialization of freshmen; it was a group in which membership came automatically to the freshman and which provided him with "viable conceptions of the national legislative process and his role in it."

What then do freshman members of the Ninety-First Congress think about the importance of voting with the state party delegation?[11] Do these attitudes change over time? Table 4 presents the basic data.

The number of references to the state party delegation as important was unexpectedly low. More than half of the freshmen said at t_1 that the state delegation was not important in their voting and only 8 of 28 assigned the delegation any major impact at all. Furthermore, there appears to be less importance assigned to the party delegation at t_2, although the numbers involved are small. The significant datum is that there was no observable trend toward bestowing greater importance to the state delegation over time as the number of votes cast by freshmen increased. No party differences were observed.

A similar finding about the state party delegation emerges from a sample of 23 freshmen interviewed by Miller and Stokes in 1958. Only 3 said that the state party delegation was either very or quite important, 10 said it was of some importance, and another 10 said that it was either not very important or not at all important. Again there were no party differences, although the number of Republican newcomers interviewed was small (n = 5). One should keep in mind that the Miller and Stokes freshmen were interviewed before taking office. Extending the analysis to the nonfreshman representatives interviewed by Miller and Stokes yields similar results, as indicated in Table 5. Here party differences do emerge

TABLE 4
PERCEIVED IMPORTANCE OF VOTING WITH THE STATE PARTY DELEGATION (in percentages)

	t_1		t_1-adjusted		t_2	
	%	n	%	n	%	n
Very Important-Fairly Important	29	(8)	38	(8)	19	(4)
Of Some Importance	18	(5)	19	(4)	24	(5)
Not too Important-Of No Importance	53	(15)	43	(9)	57	(12)
Total	100	(28)	100	(21)	100	(21)

TABLE 5

IMPORTANCE OF THE STATE PARTY DELEGATION FOR NON-FRESHMAN REPRESENTATIVES IN THE MILLER AND STOKES SAMPLE[a] (in percentages)

	Representatives						
	Senior			Junior			
	R	D	All	R	D	All	All Representatives
Very or Quite Important	14	34	27	15	29	22	25
Of Some Importance	18	22	21	26	18	22	21
Not Very or Not at All Important	68	44	52	59	53	56	54
Total	100	100	100	100	100	100	100
n	(22)	(41)	(63)	(27)	(28)	(55)	(118)

a. Members elected prior to 1950 were classified as senior representatives; those elected after 1950 were considered junior representatives.

with both senior and junior Democrats about twice as likely as their Republican counterparts to claim that the state delegation is important. This party difference appears to be due to a greater proportion of Democrats coming from homogeneous, one-party regions where deviance from the delegation position, particularly on crucial issues, can be very visible. But the primary interpretation of the Miller and Stokes data is that a relatively small proportion of the representatives interviewed said that the state party delegation was of any substantial importance.

Thus, there appears to be an inconsistency between the claim made for the primacy of the state party delegation in the studies (particularly the roll call analyses) mentioned earlier and the lesser importance assigned to it by both the Ninety-First class and the Miller and Stokes respondents. One way of reconciling these apparently discrepant findings is to argue that they are due to differences inherent in roll call and interview data. The freshmen were asked about the impact of the state party delegation independent of any concrete legislative setting which may have been the reason for the low importance granted to it. Hence, we might argue that given the limitations inherent in the interview situation the number of references to the state party delegation was actually high and not low.

While there is some validity to the above argument, a more fruitful way to reconcile the varying results is to ask how the state party delegation could be important or at least appear to be important in House voting without the representative formally perceiving it as such. Certainly one case in which the state party delegation appears to be a significant cue-giver occurs when representatives are elected from similar districts within a state. Here members of the delegation may be voting together in response to common constituency problems and pressures without any formal interaction taking place among them. One freshman Republican in the Ninety-First Congress claimed that voting with his fellow state party member was not too important, but then he added, "Since he represents a district similar to mine, I expect to vote with him most of the time." A New York freshman Democrat said:

> It's not at all important to vote with your fellow party members. Each Congressman is his own commander, his own general. However, the Democratic delegation often votes together because of similar views and philosophies, because of our common New York background.

Thus, we have here two excellent examples of where the state party delegation would appear to be very crucial in a roll call analysis, but far less so in an interview study.

Stevens (1970: 27-28) has listed five basic reasons as to why one would expect to find substantial state party delegation unity. These are:

(1) similarity of attitudes resulting from social and cultural environ-ments which are more homogeneous within a state party than across state lines;

(2) perceived similarity of constituent interests and desires, which makes deviation from unitary behavior electorally undesirable;

(3) the political and social organization of the House, which make a congressman dependent upon his delegation for an attractive committee assignment and for socialization into the expected behavioral patterns associated with House membership;

(4) the interaction of the above facts of the legislative life to produce lasting friendships, trust, and hence a mutual dependence of which one piece of evidence would be the use of fellow members to gain information on bills within their areas of committee expertise;

(5) the desire of delegations to maximize the bargaining power by fostering membership cohesion.

While all of these factors may be operating so as to produce cohesive state party voting, they do not necessarily cause the representative to perceive the state party delegation as influential or important. Only for the second and fifth reasons cited by Stevens does the state party delegation itself become salient to the congressman. That is, the delegation becomes salient to the member when he realizes that he has voted or is about to vote opposite his state party colleagues. In such a situation, potential electoral difficulties becomes pertinent to the representative, as illustrated by the following two nonfreshman responses.

> I've gone my own way. I have a reputation for being frequently off the ranch. But my district has changed, it now has shared counties with two other representatives, both Republicans like myself, and I am now more conscious of how they are voting. I like to know how they will vote and am glad when we can vote together since if we split it heightens the pressures from back home and heightens the comparing.

> It's not too important to vote with the delegation, but at times odious comparisons are made if one does not vote like the rest of the delegation. Fortunately, most of the Texas delegation votes together, not because we have a delegation caucus, but because we think alike on issues.

A closely related situation in which the state delegation assumes importance is in explaining one's vote to the district.[12] An unpopular vote that is in harmony with delegation colleagues is thought to be easier to justify to the district as legitimate. A Michigan Republican commented:

> The state delegation is not an important influence on how I vote, but it is important in explaining my vote to my constituents. That is, saying that so-and-so also from Michigan voted this way or that helps justify your own position and conversely.

Another instance in which the state party delegation itself becomes salient to the member occurs when the delegation is pushing some pet project, the achievement of which would be expedited if the delegation were unified. Only two freshmen said that it was important to vote with the state party delegation in order to make it more effective, and both of these members were from the same state, leading one to speculate that delegation solidarity was a norm stressed by the more senior members of the delegation. These two freshmen remarked:

> I would like to vote with the delegation when I can. There is a virtue to solidarity; it gives the delegation more influence.

> It's rather important if we can move as a force. It actually happens that a bloc is more powerful. Each member of the bloc enjoys more power than he did as an individual.

Two New York freshmen (a Democrat and a Republican) said that in general voting with their state party delegation was of no importance at all because of the great diversity in New York congressional districts, but did add that there may be issues pertinent to the state as a whole in which the delegation would move as a unit.

In conclusion, then, it appears that the state party delegation is an important source of cues and information for congressmen and particularly for freshmen, although there are situations in which its impact may not be consciously recognized by the representative himself. In some cases, the party delegation is a surrogate for other factors such as shared ideological preferences and similar constituency pressures. The disparate results from roll call and interview studies are most likely functions of the data employed in each and do not indicate any real inconsistencies.

THE PARTY LEADERSHIP

While commentators have bemoaned the lack of cohesive voting in the Democratic and Republican parties, the fact remains that studies have repeatedly shown that party accounts for more variance in legislative voting than any other variable. Matthews and Stimson (1969a: 23) found that after the state party delegation, the most important cue-givers were the party leaders and the House majority party. In his study of the Eighty-First Congress, Truman (1959: 246) concluded that although the elective leaders of the House did have to contend with independent seniority leaders, they did "act as if they were the trustees of the party's record." The question remains: do representatives take cues from their leadership, do they perceive that voting with the party leadership is important, or are there other explanations for the frequently observed high levels of party voting and cohesion? Table 6 gives the t_1 and t_2

TABLE 6
FRESHMAN ATTITUDES TOWARD VOTING WITH THE PARTY LEADERSHIP

	t_1	t_1-adjusted	t_2
Very Important-Quite Important	7	5	5
Of Some Importance	5	4	8
Not Very Important	14	12	10
Don't Know	2	2	0
Total n	28	23	23

freshman responses to a general question about the importance of voting with the party leadership.[13]

As one can observe, attitudes toward voting with the party leadership remain stable over time with a very slight indication of an increased importance for it. There were no major party differences among the freshmen, although Democratic newcomers were somewhat more likely to say that voting with the party leadership was unimportant. The main point to note is that at both t_1 and t_2 the most frequently given response asserted that voting with the party leadership was unimportant. This point is supported by another item that asked the member how he would vote when his party's legislative program and his district's preferences were in conflict. The most frequent response was that the freshman would vote his own conscience and beliefs first, the district's wishes second, with adherence to the party's program finishing a poor third. Finally, the freshmen were asked in which of the three issue areas (of foreign policy, domestic policy, and civil rights) it was most important and least important to go along with the party leadership. Freshmen of both parties divided about evenly in saying that foreign and domestic policy were the areas most important to be faithful in and civil rights least important.

Thus, a similar finding emerges with respect to the party and party leadership as developed when the state party delegation was the object of analysis. Roll call analyses indicate that party has great predictive power, that party leaders often lead the way in party loyalty; and yet in the interviews the importance of the leadership appears minimal. How can one reconcile these statements? One can legitimately argue that measuring the importance of the party leadership by means of a general survey question is an incorrect or, at least, an error-prone procedure; a better handle on the importance of party leadership can be gained if one analyzes a specific bill or vote. When we are asking how important the party leadership is, we are in effect asking how important it is in relation to other possible influences. Thus, the optimal bill or vote about which to inquire would be a controversial one that involved conflicting pressures, say between constituency and party. On the basis of this argument, one might conclude that the information obtained by using general queries is not very interesting or reliable.

Another argument that reconciles the roll call and survey results involves recruitment and ideology. Instead of asserting that party voting occurs because representatives follow their leaders, it could be argued that common voting patterns arise because the party attracts (recruits) members with similar ideological predispositions because of the general positions for which the party stands. Or one might argue that since the parties represent essentially different kinds of districts, the recruitment process and subsequent sensitivity to district problems will manifest itself in cohesive voting. Consequently, party voting occurs because members are evaluating bills within similar ideological frameworks or responding to similar constituency problems. In such cases, the party leadership need not be perceived as important. As one freshman said:

> I'm not going to vote for a bill because it is a party bill. But because of certain principles and philosophy that I share with my party, the chances are I'll end up on the GOP side. But I've never voted on the party side just for the sake of voting for the party.

In general, the meaning of party voting and the party-relatedness of the factors that produce party cohesion have been the sources of some controversy (Crane, 1960: 237-249; Greenstein and Jackson, 1963: 156-166).

We can now inquire whether freshman attitudes toward party voting are reflected in their roll call behavior. A shorthand way to address this query is to utilize *Congressional Quarterly* party unity scores, despite their obvious shortcomings.[14] The relevant figures are presented in Table 7.

Note that the expected patterns hold well only for Democratic freshmen. However, in both parties, newcomers who said that party voting was very important did have the highest unity scores. The mean support score of 56 for the eight Democratic freshmen who said that voting with the party leadership was not very important is a misleading figure as it masks a great variation in the individual scores of these eight freshmen. Three of the eight are from the south and their mean unity score is 31, while the other five are all activist liberals (including the three black freshmen) with an average unity score of 71. Thus, there are two types of

TABLE 7
MEAN PARTY UNITY SCORES BY PERCEIVED IMPORTANCE OF PARTY VOTING (in percentages)

	Very Important	Of Some Importance	Not Very Important
Republicans			
Unity Scores	72	65	68
n	(4)	(4)	(6)
Democrats			
Unity Scores	74	65	56
n	(3)	(1)	(8)

freshman Democrats who tend to say that party voting is unimportant: (1) southerners outside the mainstream of their party in terms of the programs and policies that they can and will support, and (2) activist liberals, upset by a whole range of issues both internal (e.g., the seniority system) and external to the House. For the former, their attitudes are reflected in behavior as measured by unity scores. But on most issues, the activist and the traditional liberals do agree so that their behavioral differences are blurred by such a gross, all-inclusive measure as a party unity score.

The perceptions that each party's freshmen have about the opposite party's voting discipline are fascinating. Republican freshmen often perceived the Democratic leadership as forcing its members to toe the line, while their own leadership was seen as less restrictive and more open. One GOP newcomer said that "Republicans don't crack the whip to force compliance." Another claimed:

> Republicans are not like the Democrats who exert pressure and force members to go along. Gerry Ford is a gentleman. You vote with the party when you can, but when you can't, it's understood.

Yet another GOP freshman stated that it was going to be easy for him to vote with his leadership. He explained:

> The leadership is careful not to force party issues. There has been one conference and that was on the debt ceiling. It's careful not to make everything into a party issue.

The fact that there had been splits within the Republican leadership itself on some issues made it less necessary to follow the party line, according to one freshman.

While Democratic freshmen did not share the Republican views about the heavy-handed Democratic leadership, they did not claim that their leadership was easy-going and casual. The more relaxed posture of the GOP leadership may reflect a majority-building strategy in which it is better to have reelected deviating Republicans than one-term party loyalists. It may also reflect a realization that heavy-handed leadership within a minority party creates discontent without holding out the rewards for frequent legislative success that often moderate discontent within the majority party.[15] The outcome of the 1968 election, however, added a new variable into the Republican leadership equation –the President. One Republican freshman commented at t_1: "I don't know what we'll face. I hear that we are usually left to our own. But now that we have a Republican President, I don't know." Although our information here is not very extensive, it does appear that the GOP leadership did begin to crack the whip somewhat with the advent of a Republican President.[16]

THE PRESIDENT

Matthews and Stimson (1969a: 23) found the President to be of lesser importance as a direct cue-giver. Among the Miller and Stokes freshmen, 32% said that the Eisenhower Administration had a great or good deal of effect on roll calls, while 37% said that its effect was very little or nonexistent. As only three of the nineteen freshmen replies to this item came from Republicans, a breakdown by party was impossible. The effect of the Eisenhower Administration was considered most pronounced in the realm of foreign policy, an altogether expected result. Our comments about the President as a possible cue-giver for the Ninety-First Congress freshmen are far more tentative and limited solely to Republican newcomers.

Voting with the President was only slightly more important to the Ninety-First class than voting with the party leadership, which meant that overall it was not very crucial. The question about the impact of the President was not asked at t_1 so that no time comparisons can be made. GOP newcomers readily admitted having voted against the President on a number of issues, particularly the IDA authorization and the debt ceiling, in just the first four months of their tenure. The most common response to the question about supporting the President was an expression of admiration and personal affection for him, coupled with a statement renouncing any slavish support of the administration. When asked whether there had been much activity by the Republican leadership to maintain a solid Republican front behind the President, the modal response was that there had not been much yet because there had been few crunching issues, although two freshmen said there had been a great deal of such activity. An examination of Republican freshmen's overall Presidential support scores by their attitudes toward the importance of voting with the President reveals only a weak relationship as indicated in Table 8.[17]

It may be that even at t_2 the freshmen were still undecided as to how far to go in support of the President. Again, a better way of determining the impact of the President on voting would be to examine a vote on which the President has staked his personal prestige yet which also involved other conflicting forces working on the representative.

TABLE 8
MEAN PRESIDENTIAL SUPPORT SCORES BY PERCEIVED
IMPORTANCE OF VOTING WITH THE PRESIDENT
(for Republican freshmen; in percentages)

	Mean Support Score	n
Very Important	56	(4)
Of Some Importance	56	(7)
Not Very Important	49	(3)

CLUSTER BLOC ANALYSIS

While the interview data suggested various patterns of cue-taking, cluster bloc analysis was also performed for two reasons: to provide confirming evidence for the interview results and to add a longer time perspective to the analysis. Bloc structures were generated for the first and second session and the first and last four months of the Ninety-First Congress. These time intervals were chosen because they represent periods characterized by markedly dissimilar legislative paces and by different levels of freshman adaptation; hence, they should prove useful in identifying changes in freshman bloc affiliations over time. A detailed description of the procedures used in the bloc analysis is given in Appendix A; it is sufficient to note here that a purposive, bipartisan sample of legislators was analyzed with emphasis placed on the blocs in which freshmen appeared.[18]

Tables 9 and 10 summarize the complete clusters presented in Appendix B. Each freshman's party, home state, and committee assignment are given; the key to the abbreviations can be found in Appendix B. If the newcomer's committee assignment changed over the course of the Ninety-First Congress, this is also indicated, along with the number of fellow freshmen and fellow committee and delegation members with the freshman in a particular bloc. Finally, the party affiliation of the fellow delegation members included in the cluster is given. Hence, in the first session of the Ninety-First Congress, freshman Representative Mikva of Illinois, a member of the Judiciary Committee, was in a cluster composed of 22 Democrats and one Republican. There were no other freshmen in this cluster; there was one Democratic colleague of Mikva from Illinois; and there were four fellow members of the Judiciary Committee.

The large number of newcomers unclustered in the last four months is due to their being classified as "missing data" because of missing more than half of the roll call votes cast in that period. The high absenteeism undoubtedly reflects the pressures of the 1970 election campaign.

TABLE 9

SUMMARY OF CLUSTERS THAT INCLUDE FRESHMEN FOR THE FIRST AND SECOND SESSIONS OF THE NINETY-FIRST CONGRESS[a]

					First Session		
Freshman	Party	State	Comm. Assign.	Party Make-up of Bloc	N Fellow Freshmen in Bloc	N Fellow Delegation Members in Bloc	N Fellow Committee Member in Bloc
1. Alexander	D	Ark.	Ag	4D	1	1D	1
2. Anderson	D	Cal.	PW	13D	1	0	1
3. Beall	R	Md.	BC	17R	4	2R	3**
4. Biaggi	D	N.Y.	MM,SA	≠	—	—	—
5. Burlison	D	Mo.	Ag,II	4D	1	1D	1
6. Caffery	D	La.	PW	5D	0	3D+	0
7. Camp	R	Ok.	II	8R	1	1R	0
8. Chappell	D	Fla.	BC	4D	0	1D	0
9. Chisholm	D	N.Y.	VA	6D	3	1D	0
10. Clay	D	Mo.	EL	6D	3	0	1
11. Coughlin	R	Pa.	Ju	4R	0	1R	0
12. Daniel	D	Va.	AS	5D	0	1D	0
13. Dennis	R	Ind.	Ju	2D,5R	0	0	0
14. Fish	R	N.Y.	Ju	17R	4	6R++	1**
15. Flowers	D	Ala.	Ju	4D	0	2D	0
16. Frey	R	Fla.	MM,SA	3D,1R	0	1D	0
17. Gaydos	D	Pa.	EL	3D	0	0	0
18. Hansen	R	Id.	EL	4R	0	0	1
19. Hastings	R	N.Y.	IF	17R	4	6R++	1
20. Hogan	R	Md.	DC,PO	17R	4	2R	4**
21. Koch	D	N.Y.	SA	3D,3R	0	1R	0
22. Landgrebe	R	Ind.	EL,DC	2R	0	0	0
23. Lowenstein	D	N.Y.	Ag	6D	3	1D	0
24. Lujan	R	N.M.	II	3D,7R	1	1R	1
25. Mann	D	S.C.	Ju	≠	—	—	—
26. McKneally	R	N.Y.	Ag	17R	4	6R++	0
27. Mikva	D	Ill.	Ju	22D,1R	0	1D	4
28. Mizell	R	N.C.	Ag	3D,7R	1	3D	1
29. Preyer	D	N.C.	IS,IF	3D,5R	0	0	0
30. Ruth	R	N.C.	EL	8R	1	1R	0
31. Sebelius	R	Kan.	Ag	3R	0	0	0
32. Stokes	D	Ohio	EL,IS	6D	3	0	1
33. Symington	D	Mo.	SA	37D	0	1D	1
34. Weicker	R	Conn.	GO,SA	≠	—	—	—
35. Whitehurst	R	Va.	AS	3R	0	1R	0
36. Wold	R	Wy.	II	3D,5R	1	—	2*
37. Yatron	D	Pa.	FA	13D	1	7D+	2*

Freshman	Party	State	Comm. Assign.	Party Make-up of Bloc	Second Session: N Fellow Freshmen in Block	N Fellow Delegation Members in Bloc	N Fellow Committee Members in Bloc
1. Alexander	D	Ark.		4D,3R	1	0	2
2. Anderson	D	Cal.		1D,1R	0	0	0
3. Beall	R	Md.	AS	≠	—	—	—
4. Biaggi	D	N.Y.		4D	0	0	1
5. Burlison	D	Mo.		1D,1R	0	2D	0
6. Caffery	D	La.		18D,2R	2	2D+	2
7. Camp	R	Ok.		9R	1	0	1
8. Chappell	D	Fla.		6D	0	1D	0
9. Chisholm	D	N.Y.		11D,1R	3	6D,1R	1
10. Clay	D	Mo.		11D,1R	3	0	3
11. Coughlin	R	Pa.		1D,10R	4	0	1
12. Daniel	D	Va.		3D	0	2D	0
13. Dennis	R	Ind.		≠	—	—	—
14. Fish	R	N.Y.		1D,10R	4	3R++	1
15. Flowers	D	Ala.		18D,2R	2	1D	1
16. Frey	R	Fla.		3D,4R	1	0	1
17. Gaydos	D	Pa.		8D	2	2D+	2
18. Hansen	R	Id.		11R	0	0	0
19. Hastings	R	N.Y.		1D,10R	4	3R++	1
20. Hogan	R	Md.		1D,10R	4	1R	1
21. Koch	D	N.Y.		11D,1R	3	6D,1R	1
22. Landgrebe	R	Ind.		9R	1	0	1
23. Lowenstein	D	N.Y.		8D	2	0	0
24. Lujan	R	N.M.		3R	0	0	0
25. Mann	D	S.C.		18D,2R	2	2D+	1
26. McKneally	R	N.Y.		4D,3R	1	0	2
27. Mikva	D	Ill.		8D	2	0	1**
28. Mizell	R	N.C.		9R	1	2R++	1
29. Preyer	D	N.C.		6D,1R	1	2D	1
30. Ruth	R	N.C.		9R	1	2R++	0
31. Sebelius	R	Kan.		3D,4R	1	2R++	0
32. Stokes	D	Ohio		11D,1R	3	0	3
33. Symington	D	Mo.		31D	0	1D+	3
34. Weicker	R	Conn.		1D,10R	4	0	1
35. Whitehurst	R	Va.		6D,1R	1	1D	0
36. Wold	R	Wy.		3D,4R	0	—	1
37. Yatron	D	Pa.		2D	0	0	0

a. Abbreviations are given in Appendix B.
Key: ≠ indicates that the representative could not be clustered with any bloc.
+ or ++ indicates that a cluster member was the senior Democrat or senior Republican, respectively, on the freshman's state delegation.
* or ** indicates that a cluster member was the chairman or ranking minority member, respectively, of the committee to which the freshman was assigned.

TABLE 10
SUMMARY OF CLUSTERS THAT INCLUDE FRESHMEN FOR THE FIRST AND THE LAST FOUR MONTHS OF THE NINETY-FIRST CONGRESS[a]

Freshman	Party	State	Comm. Assign.	Party Make-up of Bloc	First Four Months		
					N Fellow Freshmen in Bloc	N Fellow Delegation Members in Bloc	N Fellow Committee Members in Bloc
1. Alexander	D	Ark.	Ag	8D,24R	7	1R	5
2. Anderson	D	Cal.	PW	13D	1	5D	0
3. Beall	R	Md.	BC	1D,35R	3	1R++	3**
4. Biaggi	D	N.Y.	MM,SA	39D,1R	2	11D+	7*
5. Burlison	D	Mo.	Ag,II	2D	1	0	0
6. Caffery	D	La.	PW	8D,24R	7	1D	4
7. Camp	R	Ok.	II	8D,24R	7	1R++	0
8. Chappell	D	Fla.	BC	10D,1R	2	1D	1
9. Chisholm	D	N.Y.	VA	8D	2	2D	1
10. Clay	D	Mo.	EL	8D	2	0	1
11. Coughlin	R	Pa.	Ju	7D,7R	0	0	2
12. Daniel	D	Va.	AS	10D,1R	2	1D	1
13. Dennis	R	Ind.	Ju	8D,24R	7	3R++	0
14. Fish	R	N.Y.	Ju	1D,35R	2	4R++	1
15. Flowers	D	Ala.	Ju	10D,1R	2	3D+	0
16. Frey	R	Fla.	MM,SA	8D,24R	7	1D,2R	3
17. Gaydos	D	Pa.	EL	2D	1	0	0
18. Hansen	R	Id.	EL	1D,35R	3	0	1
19. Hastings	R	N.Y.	IF	6R	1	1R	0
20. Hogan	R	Md.	DC,PO	2D,23R	2	0	3**
21. Koch	D	N.Y.	SA	39D,1R	2	11D+	4*
22. Landgrebe	R	Ind.	EL,DC	8D,24R	7	3R++	0
23. Lowenstein	D	N.Y.	Ag	13D	1	3D	0
24. Lujan	R	N.M.	II	18D,20R	2	1R	1
25. Mann	D	S.C.	Ju	18D,20R	2	1D,1R	0
26. McKneally	R	N.Y.	Ag	6R	1	1R	0
27. Mikva	D	Ill.	Ju	39D,1R	2	3D+	3*
28. Mizell	R	N.C.	Ag	8D,24R	7	0	5**
29. Preyer	D	N.C.	IS,IF	8D,3R	0	1D	0
30. Ruth	R	N.C.	EL	18D,20R	2	5D+,2R++	2
31. Sebelius	R	Kan.	Ag	2D,23R	2	2R	0
32. Stokes	D	Ohio	EL,IS	8D	2	1D	1
33. Symington	D	Mo.	SA	48D,4R	0	1D	3
34. Weicker	R	Conn.	GO,SA	1D,35R	3	0	6
35. Whitehurst	R	Va.	AS	8D,24R	7	1D	3
36. Wold	R	Wy.	II	2D,23R	2	0	3
37. Yatron	D	Pa.	FA	2D	0	0	0

TABLE 10 (Continued)

Freshman	Party	State	Comm. Assign.	Party Make-up of Bloc	Last Four Months		
					N Fellow Freshmen in Bloc	N Fellow Delegation Members in Bloc	N Fellow Committee Members in Bloc
1. Alexander	D	Ark.		14D,1R	2	0	0
2. Anderson	D	Cal.		2D	0	0	0
3. Beall	R	Md.	AS	1D,4R	0	0	3
4. Biaggi	D	N.Y.		5D	0	3D	1
5. Burlison	D	Mo.		7D,2R	1	0	1
6. Caffery	D	La.		7D,2R	1	1D	1
7. Camp	R	Ok.		9R	0	0	0
8. Chappell	D	Fla.		21D,2R	0	2D+	1
9. Chisholm	D	N.Y.		12D	2	6D	0
10. Clay	D	Mo.		4D	0	0	1
11. Coughlin	R	Pa.		8R	2	0	1
12. Daniel	D	Va.		5D,10R	2	1D,1R	2
13. Dennis	R	Ind.		6R	0	0	1
14. Fish	R	N.Y.		8R	2	2R++	1
15. Flowers	D	Ala.		5D	0	1D	1
16. Frey	R	Fla.		5R	1	0	2**
17. Gaydos	D	Pa.		3D,3R	1	1D,2R	0
18. Hansen	R	Id.		1,3R	0	0	1
19. Hastings	R	N.Y.		#	—	—	—
20. Hogan	R	Md.		8R	2	1R	1
21. Koch	D	N.Y.		12D	2	6D	0
22. Landgrebe	R	Ind.		6R	0	0	2
23. Lowenstein	D	N.Y.		12D	2	6D	0
24. Lujan	R	N.M.		#	—	—	—
25. Mann	D	S.C.		2D,2R	1	0	1
26. McKneally	R	N.Y.		#	—	—	—
27. Mikva	D	Ill.		16D	0	0	1
28. Mizell	R	N.C.		5D,10R	2	2R++	2**
29. Preyer	D	N.C.		14D,1R	2	0	0
30. Ruth	R	N.C.		5D,10R	2	2R++	0
31. Sebelius	R	Kan.		5R	1	0	1
32. Stokes	D	Ohio		5D	0	0	1
33. Symington	D	Mo.		14D,1R	2	1D	0
34. Weicker	R	Conn.		#	—	—	—
35. Whitehurst	R	Va.		2D,2R	1	0	0
36. Wold	R	Wy.		#	—	—	—
37. Yatron	D	Pa.		3D,3R	1	1D,2R	1

a. Abbreviations are given in Appendix B.
Key: See Table 9.

STATE DELEGATION ALLEGIANCE

A comparison of the bloc structures over time supports the previous conclusion about the importance of the state delegation as a source of cues for the newcomer early in his tenure.[19] In the first session, 24 of the freshmen were in clusters that included at least one other representative from their home state; the comparable figure is 18 for the second session. This difference becomes more pronounced when comparing the early and final months of the Ninety-First Congress: in the first four months, 27 of the newcomers were in a delegation-related cluster versus only 15 in the last four months, a difference fully in conformity with the central role played initially by the state delegation. These latter figures are in part a function of the larger blocs in the first four months resulting from a less differentiated issue space.

While the delegation is important, its influence is not all-powerful. For example, freshman Democrat Glenn Anderson of California, a state whose delegation caucuses regularly, did not appear in a cluster with a fellow Californian in either session of the Ninety-First. The bloc structure of Abner Mikva of Illinois did not indicate any substantial links to the Cook County House delegation. Yet both Anderson and Mikva are members of highly cohesive delegations (Deckard, 1972). Even the high voting similarity exhibited by the Pennsylvania Democratic delegation (see cluster 4 of session 1 and clusters 1 and 11 of session 2) did not lead freshman Gus Yatron to appear in a Pennsylvania-linked cluster in the second session. And Democratic newcomer Mario Biaggi of the Bronx was unclustered in the first session and appeared in a minor New York bloc in the second.

All of these examples suggest the presence of factors that diminish delegation allegiance. The bloc analysis cannot tell us the reasons for this phenomenon, but in the cases cited, one likely cause is the member's own ideological predispositions. It is not inaccurate (and rating scores agree) to describe Mikva as more liberal than the average Chicago Democrat, or Yatron and Biaggi as more conservative than the average Pennsylvania or New York City Democratic congressman. This suggests, as did some of the interview responses, the place of ideological compatibility in cue-taking.

COMMITTEE ALLEGIANCE

A committee-oriented comparison gives some indication of the increased importance of fellow committee members as cue-givers with the passage of time. In the first session, 16 freshmen were in blocs that included fellow committee members, a number that rose to 23 for the second session. Between the first and last four months, there was actually a decline from 23 to 21 freshmen who were in clusters with fellow committee members, but these figures must be interpreted in light of the large-sized blocs of the first four months. The more appropriate comparison is that in the last four months 15 freshmen were in delegation-related clusters versus 21 in committee-linked blocs.

The cluster patterns of freshman Republican J. Glenn Beall of Maryland, originally assigned to the Banking and Currency Committee, provide intriguing evidence of the relevance of committee members to cue transmission. In the first session, Beall was part of a 17-man Republican cluster (cluster 3), largely eastern, that included 4 other newcomers and the ranking minority member of Banking and Currency. Beall was not found in a cluster in the full second session; but for the final four months, he was in a bloc with 4 Republicans and a Democrat (cluster 17), all from New York and Pennsylvania. Four of the 6 representatives in this cluster were on the Armed Services Committee; in the first session, only one of the 17 members of Beall's bloc was on Armed Services. The crucial datum is that Beall was transferred to the Armed Service Committee toward the end of the first session of the Ninety-First Congress. Hence, in this case, changes in bloc associations reflected switches in committee assignment very closely, again suggesting (though not proving) the role of fellow committee members as agents of cue transmission.

PARTY LEADERSHIP BLOCS

The most striking feature concerning the party leaders is the almost complete absence of leadership blocs that consistently include freshmen. For example, a GOP leadership bloc clearly emerged in the first session; it included among others Gerry Ford, Les Arends, John Anderson, John Byrnes, Bob Wilson, and Rogers Morton. But despite this Republican powerhouse, no GOP newcomers fell into this bloc. A similar situation held for the more widely scattered Democratic leadership. Carl Albert and Hale Boggs were in the same bloc in the first session, but it also included no freshmen. Thus, bloc analysis reveals there are many representatives other than the party leaders whose voting behavior corresponds more closely to that of the freshmen. This does not rule out the possibility of party leaders serving as cue-givers; it does imply, however, that the leaders are in stiff competition with other potent cue-transmitters.

While changes do occur in the freshman bloc associations over time, there are also recurring patterns. A prime example is the bloc affiliations of freshman Democrat James Symington of Missouri. In the first session,

Symington is the only newcomer in a 37-member Democratic bloc (cluster 1), that is most accurately described as the moderate-to-liberal Democratic establishment. In the bloc are 7 committee chairmen, the senior Democrats from 4 sizable state delegations including the Dean of the House, and numerous other influential Democrats. That Symington was the only freshman in this party bloc reflects the fact that the Ninety-First Congress Democratic freshmen tended to be either southerners (usually conservative) or activist, urban liberals. This suggests that the Democratic freshmen were particularly selective in their voting associations and did not simply opt to vote with the party leadership or the state delegation. Support for this assertion is provided by the persistence of this "establishment" bloc into the second session and the continued presence of Symington as the only first-termer in the bloc. Moreover, in the first four months of the Ninety-First, a huge 52-member bloc (cluster 2) appeared that included 8 committee chairmen, Carl Albert, and Hale Boggs; and yet Symington was still the only freshman in the bloc. This perhaps suggests that Symington is well situated in his party, both in voting and geography, for attaining a leadership position.

COMPLEXITY OF THE DATA

The complexity of the freshman Democratic blocs beyond simple attachments to the party leadership or the state delegation is further demonstrated in the placement of a number of liberal Democrats. Abner Mikva of Illinois does not fall in a delegation-dominated bloc in session one, but in a liberal one composed largely of DSG members. The three black freshmen—Representatives Chisholm, Clay, and Stokes—are not in the main centrist and liberal blocs of the first session, but instead form their own grouping (cluster 13) with a liberal New York freshman and 2 liberal Californians. Chisholm, Clay, and Stokes also cluster together in the second session, this time with 9 other liberal New Yorkers and Californians. The multiplicity of liberal blocs implies a variety of factors that produce voting similarities.

The southern Democratic freshmen are in radically different blocs that are much more intimately tied to their own state delegations. Of the 7 southern freshmen, 5 appeared in state-related blocs in the first session, one was unclustered, and the last was clustered but not with any member from his home state. This latter representative was L. Richardson Preyer of North Carolina, commonly described as a more moderate southern Democrat, a description mirrored in various rating scores. Preyer's first session bloc was bipartisan (cluster 7) with no other southerners; while in the second session, his bloc included 2 North Carolina Democrats, 2 other southern Democrats, a Democrat from Oregon, and a Republican newcomer from Virginia, G. William Whitehurst. In the last four months of the Ninety-First when reelection pressures would presumably be greatest for Preyer and voting with the state delegation a sound electoral strategy, Preyer's bloc (cluster 3) included no fellow North Carolinians. Preyer's atypicality, compared with his southern colleagues, again hints at the complexity underlying the choice of one's cue-givers.

In the second session, 6 of 7 southern freshmen were in delegation-linked blocs. The relative importance of the delegation for southerners is confirmed by the interview data. The modal southern freshman response was that voting with the state delegation was of some importance, while voting with the party leadership was not at all important. Undoubtedly, the distance between the state and national Democratic parties perceived by southern freshmen increased the salience of the state delegation in voting situations. Some of the southern clusters were overwhelmingly state delegation in composition. For example, in the first session, Walter Flowers was grouped (cluster 8) with 2 fellow Alabamans and a South Carolinian; in the second session, W. C. Daniel was clustered with 2 fellow Virginians (cluster 13).

Similar selectivity in bloc associations can be observed for Republican newcomers. There were clusters in both sessions (cluster 3, session 1 and cluster 5, session 2) with substantial continuity of membership that included 5 moderate eastern freshmen and eastern non-freshmen. Likewise, conservative Republican blocs that involved freshmen can also be identified in each session (e.g., cluster 12, session 1 and cluster 7, session 2), although the membership of these blocs fluctuated widely.

The most intriguing blocs to examine are those involving southern Republican newcomers. Here the relative importance of regional versus party ties comes into play: do southern Republicans tend to cluster with fellow Republicans or with southern Democrats? The bipartisan sample employed herein allows for the emergence of bipartisan southern clusters and such clusters do appear. In each session, 2 of the 4 southern freshmen fall in bipartisan groupings. Wilmer Mizell and Earl Ruth, two GOP representatives from North Carolina, were in different blocs in the first session. Mizell's was bipartisan with 3 Democrats from North Carolina in the bloc; while Ruth's was solidly Republican with 1 fellow home state representative. In the second session, both men were in the same solidly Republican bloc that included the senior GOP member from North Carolina. Virginia Representative Whitehurst clustered with Republicans from Virginia and Kansas in the first session (cluster 16) and was the only

Republican in a cluster of 7 that included a Virginia Democrat in the second session (cluster 12). Finally, Louis Frey of Florida appeared in bipartisan blocs in both sessions (clusters 20 and 9); only in the first was a non-freshman Floridian included and he was a Democrat. Perhaps the politics of region are less pervasive in a heterogeneous southern state as Florida. The major conclusion, however, is that bipartisan blocs for southern Republicans are not uncommon, a likely consequence of similar district pressures reflecting a still distinct regional politics.

Not all freshmen have the advantage of a state delegation large enough to be a source of cues. There were three Republicans in the Ninety-First class in such a situation: John Wold of Wyoming, the only Wyoming representative; and Manuel Lujan and Orville Hansen, 1 of only 2 representatives from New Mexico and Idaho, respectively. Only for Wold do the bloc structures reveal any consistent patterns. In both sessions he appeared in bipartisan blocs (clusters 7 and 6) composed mainly of western representatives and particularly Californians. Perhaps the California delegation served as a reference group for Wold because of common regional concerns. His assignment to the Interior and Insular Affairs Committee would certainly have involved him in problems particular to the western United States; in fact, his first session bloc included the chairman of the Interior Committee. Despite the lack of a major state delegation, the interview responses of Wold, Lujan, and Hansen all attributed little importance to the party leadership; useful cue-givers were generally described as members who represented similar kinds of districts or who were ideologically compatible.

SUMMARY

What then might we conclude from the bloc analysis? It partially supports Matthews and Stimson's conclusion about the importance of the state party delegation and also suggests the significance of the entire state delegation in special circumstances. The effect of the delegation may be diminished by such factors as the member's own policy preferences, especially if they are atypical of his delegation's. There is some evidence attesting to the more active part played by committee colleagues as cue-givers over time.

In general, the complexity of the obtained bloc structures strongly implied that members were highly selective in utilizing cue-givers; simple party and/or delegation allegiance was not sufficient to account for the patterns uncovered. Finally, it must be emphasized that the cluster analysis by itself has not and cannot formally prove the existence of cue transmission. But the bloc analysis in conjunction with the interview material indicates that cue-taking is a complex phenomenon that requires a learning period for the legislative newcomer. And, most importantly, the convergence of the findings from the interview and cluster analyses demonstrates that distinctive patterns of cue-learning do occur.

CONCLUSION

Throughout this paper we have been concerned with how the freshman learns cues. The basic premise was that the cue-giving model proposed by Matthews and Stimson is a highly plausible one, although it leaves many questions unanswered. In particular, it does not encompass process matters such as the development of patterns of cue-taking over time. The predominant pattern identified in the present study appears to be one of heavy reliance on the state delegation as a source of cues early in the newcomer's incumbency followed by a broadening of his cue receptivity over time to incorporate members of relevant committees. Furthermore, there were different patterns of cue-taking depending upon whether the issue was perceived in a partisan context or in an informational one.

One must decide what sort of evidence is necessary for validation of the cue transmission model. This requires a clear conceptualization of cue transmission. If it is to imply face-to-face interactions among representatives, then roll call analyses are not sufficient to confirm the model, and other types of data, such as interview material, are required. But we have shown that interview and roll call data are likely to give disparate results about the importance of various cue-givers, mainly because traditional survey techniques ask the representative to generalize about his decision-making processes. Furthermore, requiring face-to-face interaction as a definitional characteristic of cue transmission seems entirely too restrictive. But once we drop this requirement, we are left with the problem of why a representative votes with the cue-givers he does, and classical interview techniques will not be very helpful in answering this question.

New strategies will have to be adopted, both in interview techniques and roll call analyses. For the former, procedures such as Kingdon's—in which the representative is interviewed shortly after a vote about the forces that influenced that particular decision—will be useful. One possible strategy with respect to roll call votes was adopted herein: the investigation of the voting bloc structures of freshmen over time to determine whether their bloc memberships changed in any systematic fashion.

Modifications can be made in the bloc analysis by examining the stability of clusters within issue dimensions defined by factor analytic procedures or by the grouping of roll call votes according to the committees from which the bills originated. Here we would expect the emergence of blocs centered on committee ties. These suggestions would further add to our knowledge of the cue-taking process.

NOTES

1. A two wave panel study of the freshman representatives in the Ninety-First Congress was conducted, the first wave of interviews occurring in late January and February of 1969 (t_1); and the second wave, the following May (t_2). Of the 37 freshmen elected in November 1968, 30 were interviewed at t_1; and of these, 24 were reinterviewed at t_2. In addition, a sample of non-freshman representatives was interviewed after stratifying the House according to party, region, and seniority. For additional information about the interview material, see Asher (1973b). Complete details of the procedures employed in the cluster bloc analysis are given in Appendix A.

2. Matthews and Stimson have since conducted interviews with congressmen to address some of the questions left unanswered by their roll call simulation.

3. My thanks go to Mo Fiorina for pointing out the consequences of excluding HR 11926.

4. These uncertain responses contrasted sharply with the confident responses given to a series of items about legislative norms (Asher, 1973b). The fact that freshmen were uncertain about cue-givers at t_1 should not worry us about the problem of measuring non-attitudes (Converse, 1970), since the freshmen readily admitted their uncertainty rather than attempting to disguise it. Hence, the t_1 interviews provide a baseline from which to evaluate the subsequent amount of cue-learning.

5. See the later discussion that attempts to reconcile the disparate results obtained with interview and roll call data as to the importance of various cue-givers.

6. The exact wording of the question was: "In general, in considering questions that come before the House, are there other members of the House whose views you find especially valuable when it comes to making your own decisions? Who?"

7. These three general issue areas are the ones employed by Miller and Stokes in their 1958 study, although their domestic policy category was mainly concerned with social welfare. For my 1969 study, the category of domestic policy was entirely too broad and would have been more useful if subdivided into a number of policy domains such as agriculture, poverty, education, and the like.

8. Each party had a leadership contest. On the Democratic side was Morris Udall's challenge to the reelection of John McCormack as Speaker of the House; while on the GOP side there was a three-way race for Republican Conference Chairman, won eventually by John Anderson of Illinois.

9. An example of how these questions were worded is: "In the March vote to raise the debt ceiling, were there any particular congressmen to whom you turned for information and advice? Who? Why?"

10. Unfortunately, this question was not asked at t_1. The complete wording of the question was: "Now I realize that members of congress are called upon to vote on a vast number of bills, some of major importance and others of only minor importance, and that members cannot possibly be fully informed on all these issues. Let's assume that you come onto the House floor in the midst of the voting on such a bill on which you were not fully informed. What would you probably do?"

11. The exact question asked was: "How about the other members of your party from your state? In general, how important is it to you whether you vote the way most of them do?"

12. The notion of "vote explanation" is treated in detail in a forthcoming work by John Kingdon entitled *Voting Decisions in the U.S. House of Representatives.* Froman and Ripley (1970: 146) have also noted the usefulness of state delegation unity in explaining one's vote.

13. The exact wording of the question was: "On bills that come before the House, how important is it to you whether you vote the way the leadership of your party wants?"

14. *CQ* describes the party unity score as the percentage of 55 House party unity roll calls in 1969 on which the representative voted yea or nay in agreement with a majority of his party. Party unity roll calls are those on which a majority of voting Democrats opposed a majority of voting Republicans.

15. For a detailed discussion of sources of party differences in the treatment of freshmen, see Asher (1973a).

16. John Kingdon's (forthcoming) interview data, which span the entire first session of the Ninety-First Congress, strongly suggest that control of the administration led the Republican House leadership to be more active in encouraging party unity. One of Kingdon's respondents said that the GOP leadership had treated only one bill as a party matter in the second session of the Ninetieth Congress; but that in the first session of the Ninety-First, many bills were so treated. Despite the increased efforts of the GOP leadership, Kingdon's Republican respondents reported that their party leadership was not at all a factor in their vote decisions fully half of the time.

17. *CQ* describes the overall Presidential support score as the "% of 47 Nixon issue roll calls in 1969, both foreign and domestic, on which Representatives voted yea or nay in agreement with the President's position."

18. A bipartisan sample allows for the emergence of bipartisan clusters, a departure from traditional bloc analyses. The cutting points used to define cluster membership, of course, determine the size of the obtained clusters. Some of the bipartisan clusters are genuine in the sense that varying the cutting points would not noticeably alter the clusters. For example, cluster 2 for the first session (see Appendix B) included (then) Republican Ogden Reid of New York with 22 liberal Democrats of whom 7 are also from New York. It is clear that Reid was firmly embedded in this bloc and would remain in it unless the most restrictive of cutting points were employed. There are clusters, however, in which a moderate increase in the cutting point would have removed the bipartisan feature of the cluster. For example, in cluster 12 for session one, Democrats Abbitt and Colmer are the last entries in an otherwise Republican bloc and would have been excluded from this bloc had a higher demarcation been established. This does not mean that the cluster as it stands is without coherence; it is composed of members commonly described as conservative. In fact, the clusters most heterogeneous in partisan terms were composed mainly of southern Democrats and conservative Republicans, implying

that the cluster technique has identified meaningful groupings–in this case, the Republican-southern Democratic coalition which *Congressional Quarterly* described as experiencing a resurgence in the Ninety-First Congress.

19. The more comparable the situations, the more valid is the comparison of bloc structures over time. In this respect, the comparison of the session one and session two clusters is a more legitimate enterprise than the comparison of the first and last four months for a number of reasons. Identical cutting points were used to define the clusters of the first and second sessions; these yielded a total of 45 and 44 clusters respectively, with 22 and 30 members unclustered in each session–obviously very similar figures. Furthermore, the issue (factor) spaces defined by the roll calls selected to study both sessions were very similar, particularly the first three major factors which could be labelled as two "partisan factors" and a "foreign policy factor." Different cutting points were used for the first and last four months' clusters, and the issue spaces differed sharply. A two-factor space emerged for the first four months and a six-factor solution for the last four months.

REFERENCES

ASHER, H. B. (1973a) "The changing status of the freshman representative." (mimeo)

––– (1973b) "The learning of legislative norms." Amer. Pol. Sci. Rev. 67 (June).

CHERRYHOLMES, C. H. and M. J. SHAPIRO (1969) Representatives and Roll Calls: A Computer Simulation of Voting in the Eighty-Eighth Congress. Indianapolis: Bobbs-Merrill.

CONVERSE, P. E. (1970) "Attitudes and non-attitudes: continuation of a dialogue," in E. R. Tufte (ed.) The Quantitative Analysis of Social Problems. Reading, Mass.: Addison-Wesley.

CRANE, W. (1960) "A caveat on roll-call studies of party voting." Midwest J. of Pol. Sci. 4 (August): 237-249.

DECKARD, B. (1972) "State party delegations in the U.S. House of Representatives–a comparative study of group cohesion." J. of Politics 34 (February): 199-222.

FIELLIN, A. (1963) "The functions of informal groups: a state delegation," in R. L. Peabody and N. W. Polsby, New Perspectives on the House of Representatives. Chicago: Rand McNally.

FROMAN, L. A. and R. B. RIPLEY (1970) "Conditions for party leadership," in L. N. Rieselbach (ed.) The Congressional System: Notes and Readings. Belmont, Calif.: Wadsworth.

GREENSTEIN, F. I. and E. F. JACKSON (1963) "A second look at the validity of roll-call analysis." Midwest J. of Pol. Sci. 7 (May): 156-166.

JACKSON, J. (1969) "Senate roll call voting: a statistical model." Prepared for the sixty-fifth annual meeting of the American Political Science Association.

KESSEL, J. H. (1964) "The Washington congressional delegation." Midwest J. of Pol. Sci. 8 (February): 1-21.

KINGDON, J. (forthcoming) Voting Decisions in the U.S. House of Representatives.

––– (1969) "The study of legislative voting: review and original research." Prepared for the sixty-fifth annual meeting of the American Political Science Association.

MacRAE, D. (1970) Issues and Parties in Legislative Voting: Methods of Statistical Analysis. New York: Harper & Row.

MASTERS, N. A. (1963) "Committee assignments," in R. L. Peabody and N. W. Polsby (eds.), New Perspectives on the House of Representatives. Chicago: Rand McNally.

MATTHEWS, D. R. and J. A. STIMSON (1969a) "Decision making by U.S. representatives: a preliminary model." Prepared for a conference on political decision making sponsored by the Sperry-Hutchinson Foundation and the Department of Political Science, University of Kentucky, Lexington, Kentucky.

——— (1969b) "The decision making approach to the study of legislative behavior: the example of the U.S. House of Representatives." Prepared for the sixty-fifth annual meeting of the American Political Science Association.

MILLER, W. E. and D. E. STOKES (1963) "Constituency influence in Congress." Amer. Pol. Sci. Rev. 57 (March): 45-56.

MISHLER, W., J. LEE and A. THARPE (1973) "Determinants of institutional continuity: freshman cue-taking in the U.S. House of Representatives," in A. Kornberg et al. (eds.) Legislatures in a Comparative Perspective. New York: David McKay.

SHAPIRO, M. J. (1968) "The House and the federal role: a computer simulation of roll call voting." Amer. Pol. Sci. Rev. 62 (June): 494-517.

STEVENS, A. G. (1970) "Informal groups and decision making in the U.S. House of Representatives." Ph.D. dissertation. Ann Arbor: University of Michigan.

TRUMAN, D. B. (1959) The Congressional Party: A Case Study. New York: John Wiley.

——— (1956) "The state delegations and the structure of party voting in the United States House of Representatives." Amer. Pol. Sci. Rev. 50 (December): 1023-1045.

WEISBERG, H. F. (1968) "Dimensional analysis of legislative roll calls." Ph.D. dissertation. Ann Arbor: University of Michigan.

APPENDIX A

The cluster bloc analysis discussed in this paper differed from traditional bloc analyses in two important ways. First, input to the cluster bloc program was *not* a matrix of agreement scores between legislators. Instead, a more complex procedure was employed, the first step of which was the generation of a correlation matrix among a set of issues that was then used as input into a factor analysis routine.

The correlation coefficient selected was tetrachoric r as it yields an approximation to multidimensional dominance (Guttman) scaling (see Weisberg, 1968: 121-125, 174, 185-189; MacRae, 1970: 151). Thus, for each session of the Ninety-First Congress, a set of 100 roll call votes was selected by eliminating unanimous and near unanimous votes. The factor analysis of the tetrachoric r matrices produced a maximum of ten orthogonal factors as a varimax rotation was used; the factors in effect defined the issue space for each session. Then the factor scores for each legislator were generated; this meant that each congressman was now placed in the issue space. Next the distance between all pairs of congressmen in the space was calculated.

For example, let there be N factors and two legislators A and B. If legislator A's scores on the N factors are represented by $X_{1_A}, X_{2_A}, \ldots, X_{N_A}$, and legislator B's by $X_{1_B}, X_{2_B}, \ldots, X_{N_B}$, then the (Euclidean) distance between A and B, d_{AB}, is given by

$$d_{AB} = \sqrt{(X_{1_A} - X_{1_B})^2 + (X_{2_A} - X_{2_B})^2 + \cdots + (X_{N_A} - X_{N_B})^2} = \sqrt{\sum_{i=1}^{N} (X_{i_A} - X_{i_B})^2}$$

Such distances were calculated between all pairs of legislators. These distances were then normed to a 0-1 range and their polarities reversed. That is, all the distances were divided by the largest distance, thereby making the maximum distance unity; these normed distances then were each subtracted from 1. Thus, the larger the revised distance score between any two legislators, the closer they were in the issue space. It was these revised distance scores that were inputted into a cluster bloc routine.

This procedure was followed instead of the more common use of agreement scores for two major reasons. One is the expense that would have been incurred in calculating agreement scores for large groups such as congressmen. The procedure employed, while involving more steps, was actually less costly in terms of computer time, particularly since a number of subsets of issues were examined. The second reason for its use is that it yields the investigator richer information than does a simple agreement matrix. For example, one can determine what issue areas (factors) are producing distances between legislators by examining the factor scores. Thus, one can observe in which domains pairs of legislators are voting in similar fashion, while agreement scores generally lump together all roll calls making it difficult to know whether patterns of agreement differ across disparate issue areas.

The second major way in which the bloc analysis differs from other efforts is in its selection of legislators for investigation. The typical procedure in bloc analysis has been to study partisan groups of legislators for both substantive and resource reasons. Thus, Truman (1959) studied the bloc structure within parties because of an interest in describing such blocs. Furthermore, it is far cheaper to analyze a collection of less than 300 legislators than an entire congress of 435. Because of my substantive interest in freshmen and their cue-givers, a different strategy was adopted in the selection of legislators. A purposive sample was chosen that included all the likely cue-givers for freshmen that could be determined by recourse to personal judgment and results of previous research.

The most likely cue-givers for freshmen appeared to be fellow freshmen, fellow members of their state delegation, ranking members of committees, the party leaderships, and leaders of informal groups in the congress. Hence, any state delegation that included a freshman was included in the purposive sample in its entirety; likewise, the chairman and ranking minority member of any committee on which a freshman served were also included. The additional inclusion of party and informal leaders brought the sample size up to 299. Great care was taken not to overlook any potential cue-giver. For example, there were no freshmen from Texas so the entire Texas delegation was not automatically a part of the sample. But W. R. Poage, Wright Patman, and Olin Teague were included since they all chaired committees (Agriculture, Banking and Currency, and Veteran's Affairs, respectively) on which freshmen served. In addition, George Mahon of Texas, chairman of the Appropriations Committee, was selected into the sample—even though no freshman served on Appropriations—because it was thought that Mahon might act as a major source of cues because of his strategic position in the legislative process. Finally, George Bush, then a relatively junior Texas Republican, was also included because it appeared likely that he would be a visible figure to Republican freshmen from the South, in part because of his assignment to Ways and Means and his prominence as a junior Republican. Thus, a sample was selected that appeared to incorporate most of the probable sources of cues for freshman representatives.

A major advantage of this approach is that it allows for the emergence of bipartisan blocs. With the presence of Republican freshmen from the South, one would not want to select a sample that by definition eliminated the possibility of southern Republican newcomers falling into blocs with fellow southern Democrats rather than with fellow Republicans. A disadvantage of the procedure is that a non-freshman legislator plucked in isolation from his state delegation may emerge in a bloc far different than would have been the case had his entire delegation been included in the sample. But since our interest is in the freshman and his fellow bloc members, this disadvantage scarcely concerns us.

The clustering algorithm yields clusters in a sequential fashion with each cluster beginning with that unclustered pair of legislators having the highest revised distance between them, so long as this distance is greater than the minimum value set by the investigator. Individuals are added to a cluster until no legislator remains who meets the minimum distance requirement with *all* the members already in the cluster. Then a new cluster is begun. The procedure is terminated when there is no distance score between any two unclustered members that satisfies the minimum value for entry into a cluster. This procedure obviously means that the number of clusters obtained is a function of the (arbitrary) cutting points. The cutting points employed herein were such that a modest increment or decrement in them had little impact on the obtained bloc structure.

APPENDIX B

The following charts present the cluster structures for the first session, the second session, the first four months, and the last four months of the Ninety-First Congress. Only clusters in which freshmen appeared are listed; freshmen are listed first and in capital letters. The remaining members of the cluster are listed in the order in which they entered the cluster. This means that if higher cut-off points had been used to define a cluster, the members near the end of the list would have been the first ones to fall out of the bloc. Each cluster member's party (D or R), home state (standard abbreviation), and committee assignment(s) are given. In addition, an (*) by a committee abbreviation signifies that the representative is the chairman of that committee, while an (**) indicates that the ranking minority member. A (+) means that the congressman is the senior Democrat on his state delegation, while (++) refers to the senior Republican on the delegation. This latter information is presented only for those state delegations in which there was at least one freshman and in which there were at least four members of the party in question. The key to the committee abbreviations is as follows:

Ag	Agriculture	IS	Internal Security
Ap	Appropriations	IF	Interstate and Foreign Commerce
AS	Armed Services	Ju	Judiciary
BC	Banking and Currency	MM	Merchant Marine and Fisheries
DC	District of Columbia	PO	Post Office and Civil Service
EL	Education and Labor	PW	Public Works
FA	Foreign Affairs	Ru	Rules
GO	Government Operations	SA	Science and Astronautics
HA	House Administration	VA	Veteran's Affairs
II	Interior and Insular Affairs	WM	Ways and Means

BLOC STRUCTURE FOR THE FIRST SESSION OF THE NINETY FIRST CONGRESS

Cluster 1

1. SYMINGTON-D-Mo-SA
2. Kluczynski-D-Ill-PW
3. Murphy-D-Ill-FA
4. Fallon-D-Md-PW*
5. Murphy-D-NY-IF,MM
6. Rostenkowski-D-Ill-WM
7. Pepper-D-Fla-IS,Ru
8. Holifield-D-CAl+-GO
9. Miller-D-Cal-SA*
10. Fascell-D-Fla-FA,GO
11. Friedel-D-Md-HA*,IF
12. Hamilton-D-Ind-FA,PO
13. Monagan-D-Conn-FA,GO
14. Gray-D-Ill-HA,PW
15. O'Hara-D-Mich-EL,II
16. Rooney-D-Pa-IF
17. Griffiths-D-Mich-WM
18. Annunzio-D-NY-BC,MM
19. O'Neill-D-Mass-Ru
20. Giaimo-D-Conn-Ap
21. St. Onge-D-Conn-Ju,MM
22. Carey-D-NY-EL,II
23. Madden-D-Ind+-Ru
24. Hanna-D-Cal-BC,MM
25. Dulski-D-NY-PO*,VA
26. Hanley-D-NY-BC,PO
27. Price-D-Ill-AS
28. Stratton-D-NY-AS
29. Feighan-D-Ohio-Ju,MM
30. Staggers-D-WVa-IF*
31. Brademas-D-Ind-EL,HA
32. Perkins-D-Ky-EL*
33. Gilbert-D-NY-WM
34. Bolling-D-Mo+-Ru
35. Rooney-D-NY-Ap
36. Celler-D-NY+Ju*
37. Green-D-Ore-EL

Cluster 2

1. MIKVA-D-Ill-Ju
2. Ryan-D-NY-II,Ju
3. Ottinger-D-NY-IF
4. Conyers-D-Mich-Ju
5. McCarthy-D-NY-PW
6. Farbstein-D-NY-FA
7. Scheuer-D-NY-EL
8. Reid-R-NY-EL,GO
9. Diggs-D-Mich-DC,FA
10. Podell-D-NY-HA,SA
11. Hawkins-D-Cal-EL
12. Green-D-Pa-WM
13. Thompson-D-NJ-EL,HA
14. Bingham-D-NY-FA,HA
15. Kasternmeier-
      D-Wis.-II,Ju
16. Fraser-D-Minn-DC,FA
17. Yates-D-Ill-Ap
18. Brasco-D-NY-BC,PO
19. Corman-D-Cal-WM
20. Daddario-D-Conn-SA
21. Edwards-D-Cal-Ju,VA
22. Rosenthal-D-NY-FA,GO
23. Tunney-D-Cal-FA,II

Cluster 3

1. HASTINGS-R-NY-IF
2. HOGAN-R-Md.-DC,PO
3. BEALL-R-Md-BC
4. FISH-R-NY-Ju
5. MCKNEALLY-R-NY-Ag
6. Widnall-R-NJ-BC**
7. McDade-R-Pa-Ap
8. Pirnie-R-NY-AS
9. Button-R-NY-MM,PO
10. Dwyer-R-NJ-BC,GO**
11. Robison-R-NY++-Ap
12. Nelsen-R-Minn-DC**,IF
13. Mailliard-R-Cal-FA,MM**
14. Horton-R-NY-DC,GO
15. McCulloch-R-Ohio++-Ju**
16. Stanton-R-Ohio-BC
17. Gude-R-Md-DC,GO

Cluster 4

1. YATRON-D-Pa-FA
2. ANDERSON-D-Cal -PW
3. Flood-D-Pa -Ap
4. Garmatz-D-Md+-MM*
5. Dent-D-Pa-EL,HA
6. Byrne-D-Pa-AS,MM
7. Eilberg-D-Pa-Ju
8. Addabbo-D-NY-Ap
9. Barrett-D-Pa-BC
10. Morgan-D-Pa+-FA*
11. Clark-D-Pa-MM,PW
12. Pucinski-D-Ill-EL,VA
13. Hays-D-Ohio-FA,HA

Cluster 5

1. KOCH-D-NY-SA
2. Moorhead-D-Pa-BC,GO
3. Morse-R-Mass-FA
4. Whalen-R-Ohio-AS
5. Ashley-D-Ohio-BC,MM
6. Halpern-R-NY-BC,VA

Cluster 6

1. MIZELL-R-NC-AG
2. LUJAN-R-NM-II
3. Henderson-
      D-NC-PO,PW
4. Jones-D-NC-Ag,MM
5. Taylor-D-NC-II,SA
6. Watson-R-SC-IF,IS
7. Foreman-R-NM-AS
8. Watkins-R-Pa-IF,MM
9. Wylie-R-Ohio−BC
10. Zion-R-Ind -PW

Cluster 7

1. PREYER-D-NC-IS,IF
2. WOLD-R-Wy-II
3. Aspinall-
      D-Col-II*,SA
4. Udall-D-Ari-II,PO
5. Mathias-R-Cal-Ag
6. McCloskey-
      R-Cal-GO,MM
7. Bell-R-Cal-EL,Sa
8. Hammerschmidt-
      R-Ark-PW,VA

Cluster 8

1. FLOWERS-D-Ala-Ju
2. Bevill-D-Ala-BC
3. Nichols-D-Ala-AS
4. Gettys-D-SC-BC,HA

Cluster 9

1. RUTH-R-NC-EL
2. CAMP-R-Ok-II
3. Goodling-R-Pa-Ag,MM
4. Myers-R-Ind -Ag,GO
5. Broyhill-R-NC-IF
6. Dickinson-R-Ala-AS,HA
7. Belcher-R-Ok-Ag**
8. Roudebush-R-Ind-IS,SA

Cluster 10

1. CHAPPELL-D-Fla-BC
2. Andrews-D-Ala+-Ap
3. Whitten-D-Miss-Ap
4. Haley-D-Fla-II,VA

Cluster 11

1. HANSEN-R-Id-EL
2. Teague-R-Cal-Ag,VA**
3. Bush-R-Texas-WM
4. Smith-R-NY-Ju

Cluster 12

1. DENNIS-R-Ind-Ju
2. Hall-R-Mo-AS
3. Scherle-R-Iowa-EL,IS
4. Ashbrook-R-EL,IS**
5. Scott-R-Va -PO,VA
6. Abbitt-D-Va+-Ag,HA
7. Colmer-D-Miss-Ru*

Cluster 13

1. CLAY-D-Mo-EL
2. STOKES-D-Ohio-EL,IS
3. CHISHOLM-D-NY-VA
4. LOWENSTEIN-D-NY-Ag
5. Waldie-D-Cal-Ju,PO
6. Leggett-D-Cal-AS,MM

Cluster 14

1. DANIEL-D-Va-AS
2. Rogers-D-Fla-IF,MM
3. Satterfield-
   D-Va-IF,VA
4. Poage-D-Texas-Ag*
5. Fountain-D-NC+-FA,PO

Cluster 15

1. COUGHLIN-R-Pa-Ju
2. Schneebli-R-Pa-WM
3. Conable-R-NY-WM
4. Findley-R-Ill-FA,GO

Cluster 16

1. WHITEHURST-R-Va-AS
2. Winn-R-Kan-DC,SA
3. Wampler-R-Va-Ag

Cluster 17

1. ALEXANDER-D-Ark-Ag
2. BURLISON-D-Mo-Ag,II
3. Pryor-D-Ark-Ap
4. Hull-D-Mo-Ap

Cluster 18

1. CAFFERY-D-La-PW
2. McMillan-
   D-SC+-DC*,Ag
3. Waggonner-
   D-La-HA,SA
4. Long-D-La-AS,MM
5. Hebert-D-La+-AS

Cluster 19

1. GAYDOS-D-Pa-El
2. Delaney-D-NY-Ru
3. Long-D-Md-Ap

Cluster 20

1. FREY-R-Fla-MM,SA
2. Shipley-D-Ill-Ap
3. Bennett-D-Fla-AS
4. Ichord-D-Mo-Is*,AS

Cluster 21

1. SEBELIUS-R-Kan-Ag
2. Betts-R-Ohio-WM
3. Latta-R-Ohio-Ru

Cluster 22

1. LANDGREBE-R-Ind-EL
2. Derwinski-R-Ill-FA,PO

Unclustered freshmen:

1. Biaggi-D-NY-MM,SA
2. Mann-D-SC-Ju
3. Weicker-R-Conn-GO,SA

BLOC STRUCTURE FOR THE SECOND SESSION OF THE NINETY-FIRST CONGRESS

Cluster 1

1. SYMINGTON-D-Mo-SA
2. Barrett-D-Pa-BC
3. Nix-D-Pa-FA,PO
4. Eilberg-D-Pa-Ju
5. O'Neill-D-Mass-Ru
6. Byrne-D-Pa-AS,MM
7. Leggett-D-Cal-AS,MM
8. Fraser-D-Minn-DC,FA
9. Celler-D-NY+-Ju*
10. Bolling-D-Mo+-Ru
11. Wilson-D-Cal-AS,PO
12. Daddario-D-Conn-SA
13. Moorhead-D-Pa-BC,GO
14. Green-D-Pa-WM
15. Diggs-D-Mich-DC,FA
16. Madden-D-Ind +-Ru
17. Conyers-D-Mich-Ju
18. McCarthy-D-NY-PW
19. Moss-D-Cal-GO,IF
20. O'Hara-D-Mich-EL,II
21. Brown-D-Cal-SA,VA
22. Brademas-D-Ind-EL,HA
23. Ashley-D-Ohio-BC,MM
24. Cohelan-D-Cal-Ap
25. Yates-D-Ill-Ap
26. Vanik-D-Ohio-WM
27. Vigorito-D-Pa-Ag
28. Udall-D-Ari-II,PO
29. Rees-D-Cal-BC
30. Thompson-D-NJ-EL,HA
31. Aspinall-D-Col-II*,SA

Cluster 2

1. KOCH-D-NY-SA
2. CHISHOLM-D-NY-VA
3. STOKES-D-Ohio-EL,IS
4. CLAY-D-Mo-EL
5. Farbstein-D-NY-FA
6. Scheuer-D-NY-EL
7. Roybal-D-Cal-FA,VA
8. Rosenthal-D-NY-FA,GO
9. Bingham-D-NY-FA,HA
10. Reid-R-NY-EL,GO
11. Waldie-D-Cal-Ju,PO
12. Podell-D-NY-HA,SA

Cluster 3

1. Caffery-D-La-PW
2. FLOWERS-D-Ala-Ju
3. MANN-D-SC-Ju
4. Hebert-D-La+-AS
5. Waggonner-D-La-HA,SA
6. McMillan-D-SC+-DC*,Ag
7. Abbitt-D-Va+-Ag,HA
8. Fountain-D-NC+-FA,GO
9. Gettys-D-SC-BC,HA
10. Colmer-D-Miss-Ru*
11. Whitten-D-Miss-Ap
12. Henderson-D-NC-PO,PW
13. Sikes-D-Fla+-Ap
14. Watts-D-Ky-WM
15. Nichols-D-Ala-AS
16. Poage-D-Texas-Ag*
17. Landrum-D-Ga-WM
18. Foreman-R-NM-AS
19. Cramer-R-Fla-PW**
20. Jarman-D-Ok-IF

Cluster 4

1. ALEXANDER-D-Ark-Ag
2. MCKNEALLY-R-NY-Ag
3. Ichord-D-Mo-IS*,AS

4. Bevill-D-Ala-BC
5. Broyhill-R-NC-IF
6. Wampler-R-Va-Ag

7. Pucinski-D-Ill-EL,VA

Cluster 5

1. COUGHLIN-R-Pa-Ju
2. FISH-R-NY-Ju
3. WEICKER-R-Conn-GO,SA
4. HOGAN-R-Md-DC,PO

5. HASTINGS-R-NY-IF
6. Robison-R-NY++-Ap
7. Gude-R-Md-DC,GO
8. Morse-R-Mass-FA

9. Button-R-NY-MM,PO
10. Gibbons-D-Fla-WM
11. Widnall-R-NJ-BC**

Cluster 6

1. WOLD-R-Wy-II
2. Burton-D-Cal-EL
3. Edwards-D-Cal-Ju,VA

4. Miller-D-Cal-SA*
5. McClure-R-Id-II,PO
6. Wiggins-R-Cal-Jud.

7. Wilson-R-Cal-AS

Cluster 7

1. CAMP-R-Ok-II
2. LANDGREBE-
   R-Ind-DC,EL
3. Devine-R-Ohio-HA,IF

4. Ashbrook-
   R-Ohio-EL,IS**
5. Burke-R-Fla-FA
6. Smith-R-Cal-Ru**

7. Goodling-R-Pa-Ag,MM
8. Clawson-R-Cal-BC
9. Clausen-R-Cal-II,PW

Cluster 8

1. HANSEN-R-Id-EL,HA
2. Bell-R-Cal-EL,SA
3. Taft-R-Ohio-FA
4. McCulloch-
   R-Ohio++-Ju**

5. Erlenborn-R-Ill-EL,GO
6. Arends-R-Ill++-AS**
7. Springer-
   R-Ill-DC,IFC**
8.Reid-R-Ill-Ap

9. Nelsen-
   R-Minn-DC**,IF
10. Smith-R-NY-DC,Ju
11. Michel-R-Ill-Ap

Cluster 9

1. FREY-R-Fla-MM,SA
2. SEBELIUS-R-Kan-Ag
3. Winn-R-Kan-DC,SA

4. Shriver-R-Kan++-Ap
5. Patman-D-Texas-BC*
6. Van Deerlin-D-Cal-IF

7. McFall-D-Cal-Ap

Cluster 10

1. CHAPPELL-D-Fla-BC
2. Lennon-D-NC-AS,MM

3. Jones-D-NC-Ag,MM
4. Fuqua-D-Fla-DC,SA

5. Mahon-D-Texas-Ap*
6. Dorn-D-SC-PW,VA

Cluster 11

1. MIKVA-D-Ill-Ju
2. GAYDOS-D-Pa-EL
3. LOWENSTEIN-D-NY-Ag

4. Dent-D-Pa-EL,HA
5. Morgan-D-Pa+-Fa*
6. Monagan-D-Conn-FA,GO

7. Sullivan-D-Mo-BC,MM
8. Griffiths-D-Mich-WM

Cluster 12

1. WHITEHURST-R-Va-AS
2. PREYER-D-NC-IS,IF
3. Downing-D-Va-MM,SA

4. Green-D-Ore-EL
5. Taylor-D-NC-II,SA
6. Galifianakis-D-NC-BC

7. Rogers-D-Fla-IF,MM

Cluster 13

1. DANIEL-D-Va-AS   2. Marsh-D-Va-Ap   3. Satterfield-D-Va-IF,VA

Cluster 14

1. MIZELL-R-NC-Ag	4. Minshall-R-Ohio-Ap	7. Belcher-R-Ok-Ag**
2. RUTH-R-NC-EL	5. Scott-R-Va-PO,VA	8. Thompson-R-Ga-IF
3. Betts-R-Ohio-WM	6. Jonas-R-NC++-Ap	9. Williams-R-Pa-BC

Cluster 15

1. BIAGGI-D-NY-MM,SA	3. Wolff-D-NY-FA
2. Hechler-D-WVa-SA	4. Rooney-D-NY-Ap

Cluster 16

1. LUJAN-R-NM-II   2. Miller-R-Ohio-Ag,PW   3. Mize-R-Kan-BC

Cluster 17

1. YATRON-D-Pa-FA   2. Shipley-D-Ill-Ap

Cluster 18

1. ANDERSON-D-Cal-PW   2. Whalen-R-Ohio-AS

Cluster 19

1. BURLISON-D-Mo-Ag,II   2. Horton-R-NY-GO

Unclustered freshmen:

1. Beall-R-Md-AS   2. Dennis-R-Ind-Ju

BLOC STRUCTURE FOR THE FIRST FOUR MONTHS OF THE NINETY-FIRST CONGRESS

Cluster 1

1. CAMP-R-Ok-II	12. Harsha-R-Ohio-DC,PW	23. Smith-R-Cal-Ru**
2. DENNIS-R-Ind-Ju	13. Burke-R-Fla-FA	24. Dorn-D-SC-PW,VA
3. MIZELL-R-NC-Ag	14. Edwards-R-Ala-AP	25. McMillan-
4. WHITEHURST-R-Va-AS	15. Hammerschmidt-	D-SC+-DC*,Ag
5. FREY-R-Fla-MM,SA	R-Ark-PW,VA	26. Waggonner-D-La-HA,SA
6. CAFFERY-D-La-PW	16. Dickinson-R-Ala-AS,HA	27. Mathias-R-Cal-Ag
7. LANDGREBE-R-Ind-EL	17. Winn-R-Kan-DC,SA	28. Mahon-D-Texas-Ap*
8. ALEXANDER-D-Ark-Ag	18. Clawson-R-Cal-BC	29. Utt-R-Cal-WM
9. Adair-	19. Betts-R-Ohio-WM	30. Downing-D-Va-MM,SA
R-Ind++-FA**,VA	20. Bennett-D-Fla-AS	31. Michel-R-Ill-Ap
10. Belcher-R-Ok-Ag**	21. Clancy-R-Ohio-AS	32. Cramer-R-Fla-PW
11. Buchanan-R-Ala-FA,GO	22. Myers-R-Ind-Ag,GO	

Cluster 2

1. SYMINGTON-D-Mo-SA
2. Albert-D-Ok
3. Dulski-D-NY-PO*,VA
4. Hanley-D-NY-BC,PO
5. Rooney-D-Pa-IF
6. Sisk-D-Cal-A-,Ru
7. Pepper-D-Fla-IS,Ru
8. Flood-D-Pa-Ap
9. Fascell-D-Fla-FA,GO
10. Fallon-D-Md-PW*
11. Clark-D-Pa-MM,PW
12. McCloskey-
    R-Cal-GO,MM
13. Monagan-D-Conn-FA,GO
14. Boggs-D-La-WM
15. Green-D-Ore-EL
16. Garmatz-
    D-Md+-MM*,GO
17. Hamilton-D-Ind-FA,PO
18. Udall-D-Ari-II,PO
19. Holifield-
    D-Cal+-GO
20. Feighan-D-Ohio-Ju,MM
21. Delaney-D-NY-Ru
22. Rostenkowski-
    D-Ill-WM
23. Morgan-D-Pa+-FA*
24. Kluczynski-D-Ill-PW
25. Griffiths-D-Mich-WM
26. Morse-R-Mass-FA
27. Perkins-D-Ky-EL*
28. Dent-D-Pa-EL,HA
29. Sullivan-D-Mo-BC,MM
30. Long-D-Md-Ap
31. Pike-D-NY-AS
32. Price-D-Ill-AS
33. McFall-D-Cal-Ap
34. Johnson-D-Cal-II,PW
35. Friedel-D-Md-HA*,IF
36. Reid-R-NY-EL,GO
37. Barrett-D-Pa-BC
38. Van Deerlin-D-Cal-IF
39. Murphy-D-Ill-FA
40. Gray-D-Ill-HA,PW
41. Green-D-Pa-WM
42. Hechler-D-WVa-SA
43. Murphy-D-NY-IF,MM
44. Staggers-D-WVa-IF*
45. Rooney-D-NY-Ap
46. Mosher-R-Ohio-MM,SA
47. Hanna-D-Cal-BC,MM
48. Vigorito-D-Pa-Ag
49. Kirwan-D-Ohio+-Ap
50. Aspinall-D-Col-II*,SA
51. Giaimo-D-Conn-Ap
52. Jacobs-D-Ind-DC,Ju

Cluster 3

1. FLOWERS-D-Ala-Ju
2. DANIEL-D-Va-AS
3. CHAPPELL-D-Fla-BC
4. Andrews-D-Ala+-Ap
5. Haley-D-Fla-II,VA
6. Satterfield-D-Va-IF,VA
7. Rarick-D-La-Ag
8. Nichols-D-Ala-AS
9. Whitten-D-Miss-Ap
10. Bevill-D-Ala-BC
11. Hall-R-Mo-Ap

Cluster 4

1. MIKVA-D-Ill-Ju
2. KOCH-D-NY-SA
3. BIAGGI-
    D-NY-MM,SA
4. Bolling-D-Mo+-Ru
5. Yates-D-Ill-Ap
6. Roybal-D-Cal-FA,VA
7. Podell-D-NY-HA,SA
8. Hawkins-D-Cal-EL
9. Brasco-D-NY-BC,PO
10. McCarthy-D-NY-PW
11. Vanik-D-Ohio-WM
12. Cohelan-D-Cal-Ap
13. Carey-D-NY-EL,II
14. Corman-D-Cal-WM
15. Dawson-
    D-Ill+-GO*,DC
16. Eilberg-D-Pa-Ju
17. Rees-D-Cal-BC
18. Fraser-D-Minn-DC,FA
19. Thompson-
    D-NJ-EL,HA
20. Gilbert-D-NY-WM
21. Farbstein-D-NY-FA
22. Brademas-D-Ind-EL,HA
23. Annunzio-D-NY-BC,MM
24. Daddario-D-Conn-SA
25. Burton-D-Cal-EL,II
26. Moorhead-D-Pa-BC,GO
27. Miller-D-Cal-SA*
28. Celler-D-NY+-Ju*
29. O'Hara-D-Mich-EL,II
30. Addabbo-D-NY-Ap
31. Byrne-D-Pa-AS,MM
32. O'Neill-D-Mass-Ru
33. Madden-D-Ind+-Ru
34. Whalen-R-Ohio-AS
35. Tunney-D-Cal-FA,II
36. Foley-D-Wash-Ag,II
37. Scheuer-D-NY-EL
38. St. Onge-D-Conn-Ju,MM
39. Diggs-D-Mich-DC,FA
40. Ronan-D-Ill-IF

Cluster 5

1. SEBELIUS-R-Kan-Ag
2. HOGAN-R-Md-DC,PO
3. WOLD-R-Wy-II
10. Clausen-R-Cal-II,PW
11. Lipscomb-R-Cal-Ap,HA
12. Reid-R-Ill-Ap
19. Poff-R-Va-Ju
20. Mize-R-Kan-BC
21. Hebert-D-La+-AS

4. Bray-R-Ind-AS,MM
5. Latta-R-Ohio-Ru
6. Zion-R-Ind-PW
7. Thompson-R-Ga-GO,PO
8. Skubitz-R-Kan-II,IF
9. Minshall-R-Ohio-Ap

13. Bush-R-Texas-WM
14. Eshleman-R-Pa-EL
15. McEwen-R-NY-HA,PW
16. Marsh-D-Va-Ap
17. Collier-R-Ill-WM
18. Pettis-R-Cal-HA,SA

22. Grover-R-NY-MM,PW
23. Wiggins-R-Cal-Ju
24. Meskill-R-Conn-Ju,PO
25. Nelsen-R-Minn-D**,IF

Cluster 6

1. FISH-R-NY-Ju
2. WEICKER-
   R-Conn-GO,SA
3. BEALL-R-Md-BC
4. HANSEN-R-Id-EL
5. Byrnes-R-Wis-WM**
6. Widnall-R-NJ-BC**
7. Stanton-R-Ohio-BC
8. Robison-R-NY++-Ap
9. Talcott-R-Cal-Ap
10. Morton-R-Md++-WM
11. Wilson-R-Cal-AS
12. Schneebli-R-Pa-WM

13. Brown-R-Ohio-GO,IF
14. Pirnie-R-NY-AS
15. Rumsfeld-R-Ill-GO,SA
16. Arends-R-Ill++-AS
17. McClory-R-Ill-Ju
18. Erlenborn-R-Ill-EL,GO
19. Johnson-R-Pa-BC,PO
20. Springer-
    R-Ill-DC,IF**
21. May-R-Wash-Ag,DC
22. Teague-R-Cal-VA**,Ag
23. Gubser-R-Cal-AS
24. Bates-R-Mass-AS**

25. Hosmer-R-Cal-II
26. Wydler-R-NY-GO,SA
27. Conable-R-NY-WM
28. Bow-R-Ohio-Ap**
29. McDade-R-Pa-Ap
30. Ford-R-Mich
31. Mailliard-R-Cal-FA,MM
32. Pryor-D-Ark-Ap
33. Anderson-R-Ill-Ru
34. Frelinghuysen-R-NJ-FA
35. Corbett-
    R-Pa++-HA,PO**
36. Derwinski-R-Ill-FA,PO

Cluster 7

1. RUTH-R-NC-EL
2. LUJAN-R-NM-II
3. MANN-D-SC-Ju
4. Devine-R-Ohio-HA,IF
5. Wampler-R-Va-Ag
6. Wylie-R-Ohio-BC
7. Scott-R-Va-PO,VA
8. Scherle-R-Iowa-EL,IS
9. Miller-R-Ohio-Ag,PW
10. Foreman-R-NM-AS
11. McClure-R-Id-II,PO
12. Watson-R-SC-IF,IS
13. Watkins-R-Pa-IF,MM

14. Roudebush-R-Ind-IS,SA
15. Broyhill-R-NC-IF
16. King-R-NY-AS
17. Jonas-R-NC++-Ap
18. Williams-R-Pa-BC
19. Goodling-R-Pa-Ag,MM
20. Sikes-D-Fla+-Ap
21. Randall-D-Mo-AS,GO
22. Hull-D-Mo-Ap
23. Teague-D-Texas-VA*,SA
24. Broyhill-
    R-Va++-DC,WM
25. Jarman-D-Ok-IF

26. Abbitt-D-Va+-Ag,HA
27. Jones-D-NC-Ag,MM
28. Taylor-D-NC-IS,SA
29. Lennon-D-NC-AS,MM
30. Fountain-D-NC+-FA,GO
31. Watts-D-Ky-WM
32. Poage-D-Texas-Ag*
33. Long-D-La-AS,MM
34. Henderson-D-NC-PO,PW
35. Rogers-D-Fla-IF,MM
36. Colmer-D-Miss-Ru*
37. Gettys-D-SC-BC,HA
38. Ashbrook-R-Ohio-EL,IS**

Cluster 8

1. ANDERSON-D-Cal-PW
2. LOWENSTEIN-D-NY-Ag
3. Leggett-D-Cal-AS,MM
4. Rosenthal-D-NY-FA,GO
5. Brown-D-Cal-SA,VA

6. Bingham-D-NY-FA,HA
7. Wilson-D-Cal-AS,PO
8. Nix-D-Pa-FA,PO
9. Kastenmeier-
   D-Wis-II,Ju

10. Waldie-D-Cal-Ju,PO
11. Ryan-D-NY-II,Ju
12. Moss-D-Cal-GO,IF
13. Ashley-D-Ohio-BC,MM

Cluster 9

1. CLAY-D-Mo-EL
2. STOKES-D-Ohio-EL,IS
3. CHISHOLM-D-NY-VA

4. Conyers-D-Mich-Ju
5. Ottinger-D-NY-IF
6. Edwards-D-Cal-Ju,VA

7. Wolff-D-NY-FA
8. Hays-D-Ohio-FA,HA

Cluster 10

1. COUGHLIN-R-Pa-Ju
2. Dwyer-R-NJ-BC,GO**
3. Taft-R-Ohio-FA
4. Shipley-D-Ill-Ap
5. Patman-D-Texas-BC*
6. Mills-D-Ark-WM*
7. Edwards-D-La-Ap
8. Steed-D-Ok-Ap
9. Ichord-D-Mo-IS*,AS
10. Railsback-R-Ill-Ju
11. Findley-R-Ill-FA,GO
12. Smith-R-NY-Ju
13. Edmondson-D-Ok-II,PW
14. Ayres-R-Ohio-EL**,VA

Cluster 11

1. MCKNEALLY-R-NY-Ag
2. HASTINGS-R-NY-IF
3. McCulloch-R-Ohio++-Ju**
4. Shriver-R-Kan+-Ap
5. Rhodes-R-Ari-Ap
6. Whalley-R-Pa-FA

Cluster 12

1. PREYER-D-NC-IS,IF
2. Gibbons-D-Fla-WM
3. Pucinski-D-Ill-EL,VA
4. Bell-R-Cal-EL,SA
5. Fulton-R-Pa-FA,SA**
6. Hungate-D-Mo-DC,Ju
7. Jones-D-Ala-GO,PW
8. Galifianakis-D-NC-BC
9. Landrum-D-Ga-WM
10. Saylor-R-Pa-II,VA
11. Rivers-D-SC-AS*

Cluster 13

1. YATRON-D-Pa-FA
2. Powell-D-NY-EL

Cluster 14

1. GAYDOS-D-Pa-EL
2. BURLISON-D-Mo-Ag,II

BLOC STRUCTURE FOR THE FINAL FOUR MONTHS OF THE NINETY-FIRST CONGRESS

Cluster 1

1. MIZELL-R-NC-Ag
2. DANIEL-D-Va-AS
3. RUTH-R-NC-EL
4. Buchanan-R-Ala-FA,GO
5. Jonas-R-NC++-Ap
6. Dorn-D-SC-PW,VA
7. Belcher-R-Ok-Ag**
8. Satterfield-D-Va-IF,VA
9. Foreman-R-NM-AS
10. Dickinson-R-Ala-AS,HA
11. Betts-R-Ohio-WM
12. Passman-D-La-Ap
13. Scott-R-Va-PO,VA
14. Winn-R-Kan-DC,SA
15. MacMillan-D-SC+-DC*,Ag

Cluster 2

1. CHAPPELL-D-Fla-BC
2. Lennon-D-NC-AS,MM
3. Waggonner-D-La-HA,SA
4. Hebert-D-La+-AS
5. Watts-D-Ky-WM
6. Landrum-D-Ga-WM
7. Nichols-D-Ala-AS
8. Colmer-D-Miss-Ru*
9. Gettys-D-SC-BC,HA
10. Fountain-D-NC+-FA,GO
11. Mahon-D-Texas-Ap*
12. Hull-D-Mo-Ap
13. Downing-D-Va-MM,SA
14. Sikes-D-Fla+-Ap
15. Henderson-D-NC-PO,PW
16. Watson-R-SC-IS,IF
17. Abbitt-D-Va+-Ag,HA
18. Mills-D-Ark-WM*
19. Long-D-La-AS,MM
20. Haley-D-Fla-II,VA
21. Whitten-D-Miss-Ap
22. Jones-D-NC-Ag,MM
23. Thompson-R-Ga-IF

Cluster 3

1. SYMINGTON-D-Mo-SA
2. PREYER-D-NC-IS,IF
3. ALEXANDER-D-Ark-Ag
4. Griffiths-D-Mich-WM
5. Sullivan-D-Mo-BC,MM
6. Barrett-D-Pa-BC
7. Pucinski-D-Ill-EL,VA
8. Nix-D-Pa-FA,PO
9. Celler-D-NY+-Ju*
10. Brasco-D-NY-BC,PO
11. O'Neill-D-Mass-Ru
12. Rostenkowski-D-Ill-WM
13. Eilberg-D-Pa-Ju
14. Halpern-R-NY-BC,VA
15. Byrne-D-Pa-AS,MM

Cluster 4

1. CAMP-R-Ok-II
2. Bray-R-Ind-AS,MM
3. Johnson-R-Pa-BC,PO
4. McEwen-R-NY-HA,PW
5. Clancy-R-Ohio-AS
6. Goodling-R-Pa-Ag,MM
7. Burke-R-Fla-FA
8. Hall-R-Mo-AS
9. Rarick-D-La-Ag

Cluster 5

1. MIKVA-D-Ill-Ju
2. Brademas-D-Ind-EL,HA
3. Fraser-D-Minn-DC-FA
4. Ashley-D-Ohio-BC,MM
5. Dulski-D-NY-PO*,VA
6. Rees-D-Cal-BC
7. Udall-D-Ari-II,PO
8. Thompson-D-NJ-EL,HA
9. Gibbons-D-Fla-WM
10. Leggett-D-Cal-AS,MM
11. Green-D-Pa-WM
12. Cohelan-D-Cal-Ap
13. Moss-D-Cal-GO,IF
14. Waldie-D-Cal-Ju,PO
15. Tunney-D-Cal-FA,II
16. Brown-D-Cal-SA,VA

Cluster 6

1. CLAY-D-Mo-EL
2. Burton-D-Cal-EL
3. Edwards-D-Cal-Ju,VA
4. Roybal-D-Cal-FA,VA

Cluster 7

1. BURLISON-D-Mo-Ag,II
2. CAFFERY-D-La-PW
3. Andrews-D-Ala+-Ap
4. Broyhill-R-NC-IF
5. Taylor-D-NC-II,SA
6. Pryor-D-Ark-Ap
7. Galifianakis-D-NC-BC
8. Edwards-D-La-IS,Ju
9. Hammerschmidt-
   R-Ark-PW,VA

Cluster 8

1. LOWENSTEIN-D-NY-Ag
2. KOCH-D-NY-SA
3. CHISHOLM-D-NY-VA
4. McCarthy-D-NY-PW
5. Diggs-D-Mich-DC,FA
6. Pike-D-NY-AS
7. O'Hara-D-Mich-EL,II
8. Vanik-D-Ohio-WM
9. Yates-D-Ill-Ap
10. Wolff-D-NY-FA
11. Farbstein-D-NY-FA
12. Conyers-D-Mich-Ju

Cluster 9

1. HANSEN-R-Id-EL,HA
2. Bell-R-Cal-EL,SA
3. Williams-R-Pa-BC
4. Shriver-R-Kan+-Ap
5. Nelsen-R-Minn-DC**,IF
6. Arends-
   R-Ill++-AS**
7. Hosmer-R-Cal-II
8. Taft-R-Ohio-AS
9. Wilson-R-Cal-AS
10. McClory-R-Ill-Ju
11. Springer-
    R-Ill-DC,IF**
12. Anderson-R-Ill-Ru
13. Conable-R-NY-WM

Cluster 10

1. STOKES-D-Ohio-EL,IS
2. Rosenthal-D-NY-FA,GO
3. Ryan-D-NY-II,Ju
4. Scheuer-D-NY-EL
5. Bingham-D-NY-FA,HA

Cluster 11

1. FISH-R-NY-Ju
2. COUGHLIN-R-Pa-Ju
3. HOGAN-R-Md-DC,PO
4. Dwyer-
   R-NJ-BC,GO**
5. Reid-R-NY-EL,GO
6. Gude-R-Md-DC,GO
7. Morse-R-Mass-FA
8. Robison-R-NY++-Ap

Cluster 12

1. DENNIS-R-Ind-Ju
2. Minshall-R-Ohio-Ap
3. Eshleman-R-Pa-EL
4. Poff-R-Va-Ju
5. Schneebli-R-Pa-WM
6. Byrnes-R-Wis-WM**

Cluster 13

1. LANDGREBE-
   R-Ind-EL,DC
2. Ashbrook-
   R-Ohio-EL,IS**
3. Clawson-R-Cal-BC
4. Devine-R-Ohio-HA,IF
5. Scherle-
   R-Iowa-EL,IS
6. Smith-R-Cal-Ru**

Cluster 14

1. BIAGGI-D-NY-MM,SA
2. Gilbert-D-NY-WM
3. Hechler-D-WVa-SA
4. Addabbo-D-NY-Ap
5. Carey-D-NY-EL,II

Cluster 15

1. FLOWERS-D-Ala-Ju
2. Hungate-D-Mo-DC,Ju
3. Bevill-D-Ala-BC
4. Ichord-D-Mo-IS*,AS
5. Fuqua-D-Fla-DC,SA

Cluster 16

1. GAYDOS-D-Pa-EL
2. YATRON-D-Pa-FA
3. Wampler-R-Va-Ag
4. Saylor-R-Pa-II**,VA
5. Shipley-D-Ill-Ap
6. Whalley-R-Pa-FA

Cluster 17

1. BEALL-R-Md-AS
2. Corbett-R-Pa++-AS,PO**
3. Pirnie-R-NY-AS
4. Stratton-D-NY-AS
5. McDade-R-Pa-Ap
6. Fulton-R-Pa-FA,SA**

Cluster 18

1. FREY-R-Fla-MM,SA
2. SEBELIUS-R-Kan-Ag
3. Pettis-R-Cal-HA,SA
4. Teague-R-Cal-Ag,VA**
5. Mailliard-
   R-Cal-FA,MM**

Cluster 19

1. MANN-D-SC-Ju
2. WHITEHURST-R-Va-AS
3. Jarman-D-Ok-IF
4. Smith-R-NY-Ju

Cluster 20

1. ANDERSON-D-Cal-PW
2. Jacobs-D-Ind-DC,Ju

Unclustered

In this list of unclustered freshmen, only Hastings is genuinely unclustered. The rest do not fall into any bloc because they missed more than half of the roll calls in the last four months of the Ninety-First Congress and hence were treated as "missing data." This high absenteeism undoubtedly reflects election pressures, particularly for Weicker and Wold, who were both running for Senate seats in the fall of 1970.

1. Hastings-R-NY-IF
2. Lujan-R-NM-II
3. McKneally-R-NY-Ag
4. Weicker-R-Conn-GO,SA
5. Wold-R-Wy-II

HERBERT B. ASHER is Assistant Professor of Political Science at The Ohio State University. He received his B.S. from Bucknell University (1966) and his Ph.D. from the University of Michigan (1970). He is the author of a number of articles on the socialization of freshman congressmen. His fields of interest include American legislative and electoral behavior and methodology.